YOU, UNLIMITED

MIND READING THE MASSES WITH NLP

JOOST VAN DER LEIJ

Morgan James Publishing • NEW YORK

YOU, UNLIMITED

ISBN: 978-1-60037-358-9 (Hardcover)
ISBN: 978-1-60037-357-2 (Paperback)

Published by:

MORGAN · JAMES
THE ENTREPRENEURIAL PUBLISHER™
www.morganjamespublishing.com

Morgan James Publishing, LLC
1225 Franklin Ave Ste 32
Garden City, NY 11530-1693
Toll Free 800-485-4943
www.MorganJamesPublishing.com

Cover/Interior Design by:
Rachel Campbell
rachel@r2cdesign.com

Habitat for Humanity®
Peninsula
Building Partner

TABLE OF CONTENTS

INTRODUCTION

THE FIRST TIME I STUMBLED UPON NLP I HAD JUST TURNED 20.
It was a great time. I was involved in a big scam from which I suffered most dearly, and NLP seemed to provide the right way out – and a way to get everything you ever wanted.

However, after I had lost most of my money I lost all faith in NLP, because I was not able to find a good teacher, having to choose from the herd of Tony Robbins, who told all sorts of unkind stories about this "Bandler guy." I liked the NLP attitude but I failed to fully understand it. So finally, I just gave up.

Then one day – I remember it vividly – Joost, with whom I ran an entertainment company, rushed up to me and ecstatically exclaimed: "You are a Seven!"

At first, I did not quite know how to respond but he was already starting to explain. It was all about a secret psychological system called "the Enneagram" – at some point published about by some psychiatrist from Chile – and it was all a bit vague, but my interest was peaked by Joosts suggestive enthusiasm so I started reading.

I raced through the little book (Naranjo's *Ennea-Type Structures: Self-Analysis for the Seeker*) and didn't think much of the descriptions of all the personalities – until I came to chapter Seven.

I was astonished. I was blown away.

Everything was spot on. All the traits described seemed to sum up all the hard work I had done to become myself. I thought to myself: "Yes! *This* is how one should live!"

Until that time I had thought I could *make* and invent myself – but now I understood that had all been set up beforehand. Including the feeling I *was* inventing myself. "The Red Booklet" provided me with a personal research project challenging me for years to come. I was able to truly get to the bottom of things and become a *Charlatan pur sang*, a *Seven Extraordinaire*. I read every book on the subject and studied most seriously.

But then I ran into trouble. A great deal of trouble.

My funds ran out, and big men demanding lots of money were banging their powerful fists on my front door. My debts grew and my income plummeted. I turned to liquor, and grew despondent and self-destructive. I lost all perspective(s).

But then, the strangest thing happened.

Joost had returned from some trip abroad and had learned some techniques from Richard Bandler about whom I had only heard some negative stories. And naturally, being a go-getter and a know-it-all he wanted to test his skill on me. Ever since I had given up on NLP I really hadn't thought about it much, but I said to myself: "Hey, let's see what he can do! Maybe I can learn something from this.."

He must have had the most difficult session ever, because we sat there for hours while he was making all kinds of approaches to my way of thinking and I was checking him all the time continuously asking myself what the hell he was doing or trying to do. I must have resisted and discarded all and every suggestion he made, until..

Until *something happened*. I could not explain it at the time, and the process of change itself remains phenomenologically amazing and hard to put into words. But something happened.

I noticed a change in my stream of consciousness. A terrible and relentless resistance I approached my peers with was taken away and even if I didn't mend my ways immediately it was the start of something new. I might say I started to trust myself. I might claim to have discarded a bad idea about myself and about the world. I doesn't really matter. I noticed the change – and I smiled.

Now, many years later, I myself use NLP to assist friends who want to give up smoking and challenge people to rid themselves of phobias. To have a taste of change. The Enneagram offers a firm grasp of people's smaller and greater problems and their solutions and it unifies the psychiatric and existentialist models of the human mind. The synthesis of NLP and the Enneagram gives you the answer to the question what it is you need to want to change.

Consequently, I regard Joosts approach as a killer one-two punch, an excellent programme to help yourself and the ones so close to you, and I am obliged to say, mindful of the words of Zarathustra:

"Verily, the individual itself is our latest, our finest creation!"

We *do* invent, and reinvent ourselves.

Koos Vos, *Master Practitioner, Master of Science*
Arnhem, The Netherlands, August 8th 2007

WHY USE THE
ENNEAGRAM
AND NLP AT ALL?

The Enneagram is a method to label six billion people according to their personality. The reason I value the Enneagram so much is that it allows me to mind read a person the moment I know their Enneagram type. Something you can learn to do. This not only allows me to understand and predict their behaviour but gives me ample opportunity to impress them with mind reads too.

This book will teach you how to use the Enneagram for mind reading. Furthermore it will show you how to use NLP so as to overcome the pitfalls that the Enneagram predicts for each type, including your type. By going through this book you not only learn to recognize your own type, but also the types of others either openly by engaging them into a dialogue or covertly by watching their actions and listening closely to the words they use. Learn to amaze your friends by knowing 'deep stuff' about the way they act, think and motivate themselves.

We start off with the fundamental base which the World Health Organisation's ICD-10 classification of personality disorders uses. This is the basis on which the Enneagram types are formed. We'll see that not everything is covered by the Enneagram and that some behaviour is simply learned while other behavioral patterns tied up with our personality. The Enneagram model allows for many subtleties as we will see.

Once we have the basics down of the Enneagram, we'll turn to NLP. NLP is quite different from the Enneagram as we will see. We have work to do in order to reconcile those two. But once this reconciliation has been reached we can move into greener pastures and actually learn how to use NLP and the Enneagram fruitfully.

These technical parts start out with the questions that you need to ask in order to find out what Enneagram type someone has. Then we move on to NLP techniques for a happy life, but only if you want this of course.

But before I start let me make one thing clear. Reading is not learning. Reading a manual teaches you even less. Only real-life experience can teach you something. It is for that reason and that reason alone that I write to you in a very informal manner. It's the best way to ensure that your brain picks up the most important lesson in this book: the right attitude.

Many years ago, I was asked to think about an innovative drugs-prevention campaign for kids aged 12-16. The idea was to make an internet-based video game to create a virtual environment in which the kids would be free to experiment with drugs, smoking, drinking and gambling. The well-known Dutch Professor of psychology René Diekstra, a member of this team, reasoned that kids may be less inclined to abuse these things if their curiosity has been satisfied by experience, be it real or simulated.

Professor Diekstra told me to use personality disorders somehow in the game because scientific studies had shown that people with a specific personality disorder are more likely to abuse specific substances rather than others. It was important to compose the game in such a way that the kids would learn something about their own personalities and their possible predispositions to certain addictions. Diekstra showed me the World Health Organisation list of personality disorders (ICD-10). It consisted of only eight disorders, which was disappointing for me because I very much wanted to introduce the Enneagram nine types. Luckily when I delved into the ICD-10 classification I learned that one personality disorder, namely the Borderline personality disorder, was divided into two subcategories.

Fortunately, because the Enneagram was not as well-known at the time. Long before I learned about the Enneagram or ICD-10 or René Diekstra for that matter, I was convinced that every man and every woman is basically the same. We all have a brain, a heart and a pair of legs and arms (well most of us). Yet most people I knew were acting in quite a stupid way, to say it mildly. What I could not understand was how people could act like this if their biological make-up was the same?

The Enneagram showed me that at some point in time we acquire our personality and this gives us a certain perspective on the world around us. It further claims that we can only understand other people who share the same personality. People with a different personality traits have a completely different perspective on the world and there is an insurmountable gap between those two that prevents us from really understanding the other person. I finally grasped why all the other people were behaving in such an idiotic way.

In fact they weren't acting stupidly at all, but they were actually acting very reasonably. Reasonable from *their* perspective on the world. And their perspective just happened to differ fundamentally from mine. The stupidity I had perceived was born from my limited understanding of people. This realisation gave me the respect I lacked for the 'otherness' of other people. One of the treasures to be found within the Enneagram.

In my view this 'otherness' of other people is fundamental. Once you have acquired your personality the Enneagram model that I use makes it clear that there is no way of changing into a different personality type. And even though nowadays there are many versions of the Enneagram model that suggest just that, I find them at fault. The one model that I follow, called the Oral-Traditional Version, makes it clear that once you have acquired your personality you can never change into another personality. And indeed: for in the last ten years I have never witnessed anyone changing personalities. Which is a good thing. People should become who they are, not the other way around.

Now this is the absolute opposite of NLP. NLP gives you the tools and methodology to change into whatever it is that you want to become. Reconciling the Enneagram with NLP is a serious problem. Many great NLP trainers despise the Enneagram.

I actually learned the Enneagram pretty much the same way as I did NLP. In case of the Enneagram my first and last boss sent me to a course in Project Management, As part of the people skills they trained for, we got two days of Enneagram training. I remember clearly that I was a pain in the ass for the trainer. Having taught Philosophy at the university, I was sceptical to the bone. It took hours before I became convinced that I really was one of the nine available personality types in the Enneagram. What convinced me was an exercise during which I would sit on stage with four people with whom I shared the same personality. The audience was then allowed to ask questions and the amazing thing was that a guy sitting to my right started to give the answers that were in my head. Amazing.

That same boss sent me to one course after another. And with the exception of the one about the Enneagram, one was even more boring than the other. I literally fell asleep in some of them, although that might have been due to partying during the weekend I must admit. Anyway, when I left that company after one year of boring courses and started my own company, I promised myself to never ever go to a seminar again.

But a few years later, one of my biggest customers organised a workshop about a pet subject and asked me to come. How could I say no? So I prepared for three days of trying to stay awake and look interested. Anything to please the customer.

It turned out to be completely different. It was the most entertaining workshop I had ever attended. No trouble to stay awake at all. The days flew by. At the end of the seminar I asked the trainer how he came to be so much more captivating than most others. "NLP," he told me. "I use NLP."

So I decided to buy a book about NLP. Needless to say It was the wrong book (*Understanding People* by Michael Hall, but do yourself a favour and don't buy it), but at least it had short interesting stories about some guy called Richard Bandler who taught the author all kinds of mischief. I gave the bad book to a good friend and bought some good books by this Bandler guy. Reading those books brought back the good feelings of the course.

Around the same time, for the first time in my life, I lost a bid for a contract. This had probably more to do with the end of the golden nineties approaching but it made me feel insecure. Among all the courses I had followed, I had never followed a sales seminar. So I concluded I had to find out who this Bandler guy really was, whether he was still alive and training people, because he seemed to match my own rebellious nature so beautifully.

In fact Dr. Richard Bandler was very much alive and training people. The website advertising his trainings with John LaValle (www.purenlp.com) looked like it had been put together by a teenager (which I later found out was true). And it all looked very American and not so much European.

Nonetheless I took the plunge, and flew to Orlando, not knowing what to expect. Spending the night before the seminar brought many doubts. What if I am the only one who fell for it? What if it is no good? The next day, much to my surprise I found more than a hundred people waiting in line for the seminar. Boy, was that a relief. If it was all bogus, at least I wasn't the only one being duped.

Even more surprising was my own reaction. After five minutes of Richard Bandler I thought: "Oh shit, if only I had learned this stuff when I was fifteen, how many problems I would have avoided. With my parents, with friends and especially with girls."

So there you are. In two different seminars I became convinced of two opposite models, which I both use in my daily work. NLP a lot more than the Enneagram though.

This book is about the reconciliation between NLP and the Enneagram. But even more so it's about learning how to use the

Enneagram elegantly within the framework of NLP. I cannot ask you to accept this now but do go out and test it for yourself. Only your own experience can tell you whether this is valuable or not. One hint though: in my view the Enneagram is on a par with Virginia Satir's stress responders which are used sometimes in NLP. Only the Enneagram model is more encompassing and more eloquent.

I know that many of my good friends in the field of NLP are missing out on the benefits of the Enneagram. It is for those people that I write this book. But others can reap the same advantages as well, for the more I study the relationship between clients coming in for personal change work, the Enneagram and personality disorders, the more evidence I find for the importance of looking at someone's personality.

This allows me to better predict future behaviour of clients and future pace them through these experiences. Take for example the case of a Type II, Helper (Borderline, emotional type). She came to she me because she had strong emotional flares and felt depressed most of the time. As soon as she entered the room I had a strong impression she was indeed a Helper. This was soon confirmed after she had done the test. Knowing this I told her many stories of how other Borderline Emotional types had reacted to NLP. How they would be great at the techniques now, but would falter in a few days and give up. But also that it would be easy to start to feel good again once she realised that it was only one bad day or even less.

And like clockwork she called me indeed after three days saying that she was unable to stop the negative feeling and feel good again. As soon as I told her that it was exactly what I had predicted and I told her to remember how easy it would be to feel good again, she started to laugh and indeed felt good. A fine example of how knowledge of someone's personality helps you with coping with their specific behaviour.

This is why I use the model of NLP and the Enneagram together. It enables me to make long lasting changework rapidly. It gives me a lot of information about the client and his or her current problems fast. As I mentioned before, the traditional Enneagram model assumes that once you have chosen or acquired your personality you are stuck with it for the rest of your life. The only changes that you can make is to become either a more healthy or a less healthy version of your personality. Making people healthier is an excellent way to describe the benefits of NLP

In this book I will cover three topics. First, I discuss the mapping of the Enneagram onto the WHO ICD-10 classification personality disorders, and its implications for NLP. The second is the best method to establish what character type someone has and how you weave that into your conversations in a convincing way. And finally the third is how to use all this in influential situations like sales, therapy or persuasion.

A fair warning though. The difference between NLP and the Enneagram is that the former is mostly positive, the latter mostly negative. The traditional Enneagram focuses more on what goes wrong than on what could go right. The following list of personality disorders I will present is downright depressing. This never bothers me though, because I am able to keep a good feeling spinning while working with all this Fraudian negativity. An NLP skill, I will discuss in time, that comes in handy at times like these. In fact, when I look at the descriptions of these personalities, I do it with a sense of humour. They only display our silliness, nothing more. Once you accept that being silly is in fact a good thing and that giving up on seriousness actually improves your life, you too can look at these disorders and laugh at them like me. We are all human, all too human after all.

DETERMINING

YOUR

ENNEAGRAM TYPE

The first thing up is to establish your own Enneagram type and learn how to help other people find their own Enneagram type though. In my view you are the only one who can determine which type you really are. No pen and paper test nor anyone else can do that for you for the simple reason that you and you alone know what it is like to be you.

The reason that pen and paper tests don't work is that most systems score on all Enneagram types and then you "are" the one with the highest score. This is wrong. You establish someone's

Enneagramtype by finding the one they identify themselves with. At the same time you make sure that he or she is certain that he or she isn't any of the other eight. In other words you have a very strong sense of recognition with one type and at the same time you are sure that none of the other eight types come even close[1].

As it can not be done by pen and paper tests three other ways remain. The first: you give the client a bunch of descriptions of the Enneagram types and you let him or her study these. The second is asking relevant questions in an open dialogue with the sole purpose of finding out the Enneagram type. And the third is that you keep your eyes and ears open to notice tell-tale signs and covertly ask test questions now and then.

The first method doesn't suit my impatient personality style so I never use that. It takes too much time and is too much work for the participant. The third I only use whenever I can't use the second (in business dealings for instance). So I use the second method mostly and rightly so.

The second method is ideal to combine with any other NLP techniques because it allows you to ask all these great (and some not so great) questions that give you more information about the client. Not just about their character, but about their situation in general and their problems specifically. Whenever I hit upon something relevant, most of the time I jump on it and work with

---

1   With the exception of type IX, the Mediator, who ,we will see, is so good at realising the worth of other perspectives that he or she will recognise themselves in a lot of different types.

that item[2], or I make a mental note and return to the topic later on. So the Enneagram is not something set aside, but an integrated part of the whole.

Most questions are designed to trigger a specific response in one type while all the other types would react differently. Most of the time this is structured around yes/no questions. However, in practice, even for a question designed for one specific Enneagram type to answer yes to and all the others to say no, you will often get that other types say yes aswell (for a variety of reasons). This is one of the reasons that pen and paper tests don't work. And this is also the reason why NLP practitioners are so much better at it than others who use the Enneagram. You have to pay attention to the way in which they say yes or no. As explained, that is where they can't help themselves but show you their true colours. It's not the answer itself that you are interested in but the way in which they give you the answer. There are thousands of ways to say yes or no.

Whenever someone says yes in such a way or tone that it displays insight and strong recognition, this is a strong sign that you are on the right track. Weak, doubtful and insecure answers are weaker signs but are not to be dismissed.

Luckily the correct approach to establishing the Enneagram types includes some pretty good tests to see whether you are correct or not. Or I should say whether your client is correct or not. I rather

---

2   Fragmentation and looping back and forth between different subjects is a great way to induce a mild trance state in the other person which helps influencing them greatly.

think of this as being a process in which you help your client find his or her own type, rather than you finding it for them. Let them do all the work.

It is also good to realize that the Enneagram is a bit more dynamic than I have suggested up till now. I like to present the case for eternally fixed and unchangeable personalities as black and white as I can. That is where the model gets its strength. In daily practical use it turns out that the Enneagram is more dynamic than just nine personality types. There is a whole chapter about these variations. For now it suffices to know that due to these subtleties people can react positively to questions meant for other Enneagram types than their own. None of this is that important as long as you realize this while asking the questions. Take your time and at some point you will hear the shift in the tone of their voices towards recognition.

Again, the object of the questions is to find out the one type that your client has a strong sense of identification with, and at the same time eliminate all the other types as possible candidates. It is also good to note that most of the time you start with a trick question which is used to set up the client for the next one.

But before we start let me make clear that the name of each of the Enneagram types is misleading to say the least. It is meant for people to recognise themselves in it, not to fit the content. Take a look at these titles and descriptions:

- The Perfectionist is never perfect. That is what makes him or her so angry.

- The Helper never really helps. He or she just seeks love and attention.

- The Successful Worker is neither working nor successful. He or she just builds an image of success.

- The Romantic is a cold-hearted materialist.

- The Analyst is not very good at analysing because with every serious analysis he or she would have noticed that at some point in time real action is required.

- The Loyalist isn't really loyal, he or she is just too scared not to make friends

- The Hedonist isn't enjoying life, he or she is running away from it

- The Boss isn't really the boss; he or she's only a bully used by others to get things done.

- The Mediator isn't really mediating; he or she is just too much frustrated about people disturbing his or her peace.

Others have noticed this too and started to come up with new names for the types. This is wrong. It's important for people to learn that the label is not the thing labelled. With this out of the way we can start the process of discovering which type you are and how you can learn to find out what types other people are.

TYPE I, THE PERFECTIONIST

Some people try to confuse the client (in case of previous knowledge about the Enneagram) by mixing up the types. I think that you should make it as easy as possible for yourself. Just go from one to nine.

FIRST QUESTION: Are you a perfectionist? [A lot of people who really aren't perfectionists answer yes to this question anyway. You are looking for the ones that give a firm, grumpy yes, start explaining that they are really, really, really perfectionist or that it used to be even worse. This last one is a phrase to look out for, as it indicates that someone has moved away from being unhealthy to being healthier. If someone says no, eliminate him or her for type I.]

Ask the people who said yes the second question: *Such a perfectionist that it becomes unhealthy?* [Most people now say no. For anyone saying yes there is a strong indication that they are type I.]

TEST QUESTIONS (use these if you have a strong indication but want more "proof". Only ask people who haven't been eliminated yet).

- *If something has to be done right, do you need to do it yourself?* [yes or used to is a good indication.]

- *The bar lies pretty high in your case, right? If you happen to pass it anyway, are you happy with yourself or does it only mean that the bar lay too low?* [bar too low is a good indication]

- *If something fails, do you get angry with yourself first and then, if it becomes too much, angry at others too?* [yes is a clear indication for type I]

Please note that many people would say yes to these test questions but you only ask people who answered yes to the first two significant questions. A yes here and there is of no importance, the only thing that matters is a strong sequence of yes's with none or only a few no's.

TYPE II, THE HELPER

FIRST QUESTION: *Do you like to help others?* [Most people answer yes, if they say no it's a definite elimination]

SECOND QUESTION: *If you help someone do you expect anything in return?* .... [you build in a pause here to give the client an opportunity to answer, most people will answer no - the liars. You wait for this no before continuing. If you see the client struggling this is a weak indication for type II.]

SECOND QUESTION continued: .... *Like love and attention?* [most people will answer yes. It's a case of how strong the yes is. If it is more like: "well yeah of course I would like some kind of recognition" that would not be an indication. You want to hear "YES!"]

TEST QUESTIONS:

- *Are you sometimes too proud to admit that things don't go so well?*

- *If someone time and time again doesn't return love and attention for your help, do you put him or her in the out-group?* [The point here is to check whether the concept of an "out-group" rings any bells. Most people don't like to be taken advantage of but are ignorant or clueless of what an "out-group"[3] would be. Helpers on the other hand …]

- *Do you have a negative self-image and do emotions overwhelm you sometimes?* [you are looking for the combination of the two. Helpers tend to cry a lot, at home, alone]

TYPE III, THE SUCCESSFUL WORKER

FIRST QUESTION: *Do you have emotions?* [Trick question to set up the second question. Everyone answers yes.]

SECOND QUESTION: *How do you deal with them?* [Any verbal

---

3   The out-group is for people who are out of favour.

answer is a strong sign for elimination. Every positive answer is an elimination. Even negative answers like "badly", "I don't know" or even "not" are strong signs for elimination. What you are looking for is someone who is totally aghast. At a complete loss for words. Guttural sounds, but unable to form words. In those cases: a very strong indication for type III.]

TEST QUESTIONS:

- *Do you play different roles in different environments?*

- *Are you able to sense when your presentation falls on deaf ears and are you able to rectify the situation by changing your story?*

- *Do you feel that it is important to be successful?*

TYPE IV, THE ROMANTIC

FIRST QUESTION: *Do you want to be special?* [Ignore the answer but look at your client's clothes. Is he or she dressing to impress and make the statement "look at me, I am special"?]

SECOND QUESTION: *Let's say that some co-worker does the same job you do, but gets paid more. Do you have a jealous feeling that you want that money too? It's not that you don't want him or her to have it, it's just that you want it too.* [A bit elaborate, but you have to be careful here as Romantics don't like the fact that they are quite jealous of materialistic gains of others. Look carefully to see how your client reacts to "a jealous feeling" and "I want it too". Especially if someone affirms that last statement, you have a strong indication for a type IV.]

TEST QUESTIONS:

- *If you walk in a forest or on a beach, do you feel a strong and overwhelming feeling of being in tune with nature?*

- *Do you have strong feelings for people who are away?*

- *Do you have high ideals?*

TYPE V, THE ANALYST

FIRST QUESTION: *When you enter a room with people, do you tend to stand aside and analyse the situation first?* [Pay a lot of attention to the way he or she looks and answers. They tend to think some time before answering and look introverted. Also type V's are least likely to want to participate in an Enneagram test. They want to hide their detachment from others.]

SECOND QUESTION: *If I were to give you a new job with a big salary, expensive car, laptop, etcetera, would you take it, even if you knew that it meant working a lot of hours and doing what you were told to do?* [You are looking for a strong "no way" reaction. Analysts would never sacrifice their personal freedom for material gains. In fact they do the opposite.]

TEST QUESTIONS:

- *Do you value your own personal freedom so much that you even keep personal relationships at a distance out of fear of being swallowed up in the relationship?*

- *If you are presented with a problem, do you look for the solution in books and on the internet?*

- *Do you want to study a subject first so as to understand it perfectly before putting yourself into action?*

TYPE VI, THE LOYALIST

FIRST QUESTION: *Do you have a lot either of doubts in your private life or professionally or both?* [Same as with type V, type VI is a thinker so he or she will think about the answer and hesitate about it. The question is a little elaborate because you want to spot the anti-phobic type VI, too. It seems every Enneagram has some kind of anti-type, which I will discuss in the chapter about variations. Most anti-types differ only slightly from the main types, with the exception of the Loyalist where the denial-type can act bravely in face of the doubts and dangers he or she sees. Most of the time they manage to act this way for only one half of their lives. So doubt creeps in either in their business life or personal life.]

SECOND QUESTION: *Are you keeping track of the social ladder and if you do, do you respect authority while at the same time rebelling against it?* [Most telling for type VI is that they are so very conscious of hierarchies. And so ambivalent towards them. On the one hand they try to rise up as high as they can on the social ladder but on the other hand they want to stand up against authority.]

TEST QUESTIONS:

- *When you give your friendship do you only do that after some time to see what the other person is like but when you do so, it's for life?* [Checking the Loyalist famous loyalty. Even if they only act this way out of fear.]

- *When presented with a problem, do you ask other people how they would solve it but in the end you'll come up with your own plan?*

- *Do you like to have a theoretical model of any situation so you'll have more grip on it?*

TYPE VII, THE HEDONIST

FIRST QUESTION: *Do you have any problems?* [Most people will say yes or begin telling about their problems. Type VII will look at you as if he or she doesn't understand you and asks: "problems?" or he or she will answer yes but very weakly. Of course any strong No followed by a good laugh is a strong indication that it is a type VII. In the case of not understanding or the weak yes, "explain" the question like: "Well, do you experience problems as problems or are problems things other people have?" and stress "other". If he or she starts to explain that this is the case, it's a strong indication that you have a type VII.]

SECOND QUESTION: *Let's say that two friends of yours give two parties some distance apart from each other. Would you go the extra mile just to make sure that you go to both parties?* [Any planning to make compromises to be able to attend both parties is a strong indication.]

TEST QUESTIONS:

- *If a friend organizes an event and you are unable to attend, are you afraid that you'll miss out on something?*

- *Are you capable of theorizing about some grandiose scheme and you'll still sell it enthusiastically to others who do not fully understand it anyway?*

- *Do you like to play around? [Which you can actually test if he or she says yes by poking and tickling him or her. If he or she jumps right in and returns the favour, it's a strong indication that you have a type VII on your hands.]*

TYPE VIII, THE BOSS

FIRST QUESTION: *If you are standing in line and you see that a little girl is being crushed in the crowd, are you going to take physical action (like pushing people aside) to save her?* [Most people would help my little girl but only type VIII would really start a fight over her. So the key here is whether they would take physical action.

SECOND QUESTION: *Well, you know how we all have our own truths and so on, right? But don't you really think that your viewpoint of reality is really more realistic than that of others?* [Look for any reluctance to go along with the first line. Type VIII really doesn't agree with this line, but they'll go along to try to fool you. And a strong agreement after the cat is out of the bag.]

TEST QUESTIONS:

- Well, the best test is physical. Just stand up and walk over to the other person and give him or her a moderate push. And be prepared to duck. Remember these are the emotionally unstable – impulsive types. You look for people that hit back or push you. Or who state that they used to be aggressive, but they now have things under control.

- Another physical test. Just stand really really close to them and ask them whether they are annoyed by it. Type VIII hates it.

- *Do you feel relieved after you have had arguments with someone?*

TYPE IX, THE MEDIATOR

FIRST QUESTION: *Are you strongly opinionated?* [Mediators see so much value in other people's standpoints that they acquire few opinions for themselves.]

SECOND QUESTION: *Do you tend to put things off, only to work up a lot of energy just before the deadline and then get it finished just in the knick of time?*

TEST QUESTIONS:

- *If you see an old lady fall, do you rush to her side to help her?*

- This one is more an observation test. If you have been going nuts so far in the test because your client either scores on all or most Enneagram types but never completely for 100%? Then chance has it that you have a type IX in front of you. Because they see value in other people's viewpoints they tend to score well on all types. Still, they are not really convinced and react much more strongly and positively to the type nine questions.

- *Do you feel relaxed when the normal things of life (partner, home, a job) are taken care of?*

Okay, so now you have finished the questions and tests. And if you are any good at this (and you will be after practising with and learning from more and more people), you'll have eliminated about five or six of the types and are wondering about three or four, most of the time with one or two really good candidates and one or two less good candidates.

Luckily, we have some unexplainable magic trick to check which one is the right one. This due to the fact that each Enneagram type is connected to other types in the following mysterious way:

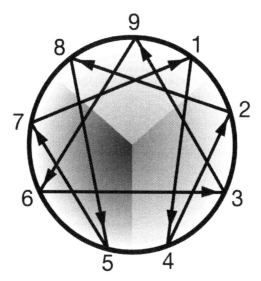

Thus type I connects to IV which connects to II, followed by VIII, V, VII and back to I. And there is another circuit, namely type III connects to IX followed by VI. Now there are many theoretical explanations why this should be the case. I found them all lacking and devoid of any practical use. In fact, the only practical use I have for such explanations of the Enneagram is as a test to see whether the teacher in question is a charlatan or not. I think that if people don't know the answer they should simply say "I don't know". Not knowing is not a disgrace but in fact knowing that you don't know is a virtue.

These lines represent the responding patterns of stress and relaxation. They work as follows: whenever an Enneagram type is put under pressure or in a stressful environment, feels tension or experiences stress, he or she will borrow the negative traits from the Enneagram type next in line. Whenever an Enneagram type is relaxing and in a calm and quiet environment, then the opposite will happen: he or she will borrow the positive traits from the previous type in line. So to double-check whether someone is one type rather than another, you check to see whether they fit the stress and relaxation responses.

Let me put that in a nice table for you:

Enneagram type	Negative borrowings in times of stress	Positive borrowings in times of relaxation
Type I, the Perfectionist	Emotional drama from type IV, the Romantic	Enjoyment of Life from type VII, the Hedonist
Type II, the Helper	Bossing around in a negative way from type VIII, the Boss	Enjoying the beauty of nature from type IV, the Romantic

Type III, the Successful Worker	Putting the things off that need to be done, from type IX, the Mediator. Or, alternatively, doing any job that does not matter rather than the one that is causing the stress.	Becoming a very loyal friend, from type VI, the Loyalist
Type IV, The Romantic	Attention Drama Queen, from type II, the Helper	Working hard and well, from type I, the Perfectionist
Type V, the Analyst	Escaping from real life by partying, from type VII, the Hedonist	Taking the lead, from type VIII, the Boss
Type VI, the Loyalist	Superficially hiding behind masks while going for the dollars, from type III, the Successful Worker	Hard work and a helping hand, from type IX the Mediator
Type VII, the Hedonist	Petty perfectionism in a grumpy manner, from type I, the Perfectionist	A relaxing solitary moment with a good book for example or a private walk, from type V, the Analyst
Type VIII, the Boss	The "leave me alone, I am angry" confinement, from type V, the Analyst	Let me use my powers to help you out, from type II, the Helper
Type IX, the Mediator	"What should I do now" doubt, from type VI, the Loyalist	Initiating new business, from type III, the Successful Worker

The only way to really learn these distinctions thoroughly is to study the people around you: your family, your friends and colleagues. So let me give you some real life examples from my own life.

First of all Arjen, my former business partner. He is a type I, Perfectionist. In times of stress he would become emotional, and then in his emotions he would move away from all the musts in his life and go towards finding out what he really wanted. And on the other hand he would find relaxation in the enjoyment of Thailand.

Jonathan, a type II Helper, is one of my best friends. In times of stress he can suddenly become very aggressive and demand that we do whatever he wants to do. On the other hand, going to art house movies is one of his favourite ways to relax.

As I am a type III, the successful worker, in times of stress I tend to become very lazy and I will just lay on the couch and watch TV. Studying philosophy on the other hand brought a lot of relaxation.

Jeanine, my ex-girlfriend, is a type IV, Romantic. Whenever we fought, she would get over-emotional and demand a lot of attention to her suffering. Then again: she relaxes when she is working hard and disciplined with asylum seekers.

Mike, another good friend, is a type V, Analist. When his relationship broke up he spent a lot of time in bars and clubs. On the other hand, when he relaxes he becomes an active leader directing us.

My father is a type VI, Loyalist. He used to work for a large bank and with each reorganisation he would play his role and focus on securing his income. Whereas whenever he relaxes he will be very helpful and active.

Koos, a type VII, Hedonist, is another great friend. In times of stress he tends to start to clean up all the irrelevant parts of his home in a foul mood. Walking through the Himalayas all by himself, relaxed him very much, though.

Bas, a type VIII, Boss, another friend of mine who in times of stress looks for solitude and something irrelevant to do. Whenever you'll interrupt him you get a remark that you should leave him alone. When he is in the middle of a group helping people he starts to relax. Martijn, a type IX, Mediator and yet another great friend, starts to doubt and ponder a lot. He will become suspicious of others in times of stress. But when he starts to initiate new projects and focuses on results rather than theories he find relaxation.

It's important to explain how not to use this table. Whenever a type borrows a trait from another type (positive or negative), it doesn't mean they become like the other types. In fact, it will not even resemble the way other types do their own thing. Each type will use borrowed traits from other types in their own manner and will display their own typical behaviour that just happens to be borrowed from someone else. Like when each different director directs the same play and it will look completely different.

Now the way to test to see which Enneagram type someone

really is (or which model fits him or her best), you have to check to see whether they recognize themselves in the corresponding stress and relaxation behaviour. Only one definite type will fit when you recognize a) the type itself, b) the stress related behaviour and c) the relaxation related behaviour. That is your real Enneagram type.

ENNEAGRAM
TYPE TRAITS

N ow that you know your Enneagram type, it is good to start to learn about your own type and the other types. Which traits does each Enneagram type have. But before I give you an overview of the most common traits of the Enneagram let me explain to you how you can learn which traits fit which Enneagram types best. You cannot really learn them from a book. Every description I have read by well-known authors rings some bells but certainly doesn't match my experience.

This is not the authors' fault but due to the fact of the ways in which language works. Any NLP practitioner will be familiar with the meta-model. When an author tries to express his or her thoughts in a book this endeavour is bound to generalize, distort and delete. This is failing in the sense that no author ever succeeds in putting exactly the right meaning into the words that the book consists of. The text just suffers too much from deletion, generalization and distortion.

Then the reader steps in. He or she too starts to delete, generalize and distort the meaning of the book. Hence, when it comes to the Enneagram types the descriptions of the traits sound familiar but do not match my or your experience.

So the only correct way to learn about the Enneagram is to write your own book, or in a simpler way, to build up your own expertise from your own experiences. As I stated above, the real experts on any type are the people of the Enneagram type themselves. So each time you meet and speak to someone, you are talking to an Enneagram master if only for just one type. The best way to learn the Enneagram is to learn it from these masters. Books like these can only show you some signs as to what to look for and what to ignore.

What you should do, is use this bare skeleton and start putting flesh on these bones by learning from everyone you meet. Notice what behaviour happens to be found within a specific type. If there is a high correlation, then you probably found a trait. If not, ignore it. The Enneagram is not about everything. In fact it is about a very limited set of traits. Traits that happen to belong to a certain Enneagram type but are not logically connected. It's about how people act, not about who they are.

Often people come to me and ask me to what type any given trait fits. Most of the time I'll tell them "none" because a lot of traits do not fit the Enneagram model. By learning from everyone you meet, you'll gain the understanding of which fit and which don't. The point of the Enneagram is not to tell it all, but to show you a direction to a happier and healthier way of life.

The following list of traits is based on Claudio Naranjo's book *Character and Neurosis*. Naranjo is the best author on the Enneagram and a psychiatrist. So I both love and hate him. In spite of the fact that I do not agree very much with his description of the traits themselves, the list is excellent. I can only give you the traits by name and with a short description because I feel all this doesn't suffice anyway. You can look up more descriptions if you want to, but the best way is to go out, experiment and find out yourself.

Type I, the Perfectionist's traits	My Short Description:
Anger	Perfectionist gets angry very quickly. What happens is that they wake up each morning and see how perfect the word could be but within seconds realize that, just like yesterday, it isn't as wonderful as it could have been and that it is all their fault. So they start by getting angry at themselves. But soon they'll think "hey, wait a minute. It's not just my fault. It's your fault too!" And then they get angry at you too. It's like a pressure cooker. The pressure builds up and up and suddenly it explodes. Even though type I people tend to think that they are reasonable and calm, the other party involved thinks World War III has just erupted. Perfectionists tend to underestimate their own aggression.

Criticality	If you always know things better, you tend to become a bit critical. Not just of others, but of yourself, too.
Demandingness	The operative word for perfectionists is "must". The world must become perfect. You must do as they tell you. It's hard for a perfectionist to get in touch with what he or she wants. Most of the time this is translated into what "must" be done, rather than into admitting it's just what they want.
Dominance	Aggression, criticality and demandingness are aspects that almost automatically lead to someone who wants to dominate the situation. Eh, I mean must dominate it for our own good, or so a Perfectionist would tell you.
Perfectionism	Obvious for Perfectionists. But note that Perfectionists are hardly ever perfect. Let alone for themselves. If they achieve their own level of expectation, they won't be satisfied but will just raise the bar.
Over-Control	Perfectionists want to control everything. If they don't do things themselves, it won't be done as well as it possibly could. So they must be in control. Of course they do have everything under control except for this tendency to be in control. That is totally out of control. It freaks them out when you point this out to them.

Self-Criticism	Realize, whenever a Perfectionist criticises you, that he or she has done this to himself or herself twice over. They are their own critics first of all.
Discipline	Perfectionists are hard workers, if the people around them work hard, too. They can be very disciplined.

Type II, the Helper's Traits	My Short Description:
Pride	Helpers won't easily admit that they are proud. They are just too proud to admit it. Same with feeling bad, they won't admit it out of pride. One of the reasons most Helpers tend to cry secretly when they are alone at home.
Love Need	Helpers tend to have a desperate need for love. That's the reason they help you so much. Just to feel loved. Easiest way to satisfy a Helper? Just hug him or her and pat him or her on the back. He or she will be most pleased.
Hedonism	Helpers like to experience pleasure. Whether it's sexual, drinks or festivities, they like to have fun.

Seductiveness	Another way that Helpers tend to satisfy their hunger for love and attention is to be seductive. Go out with a Helper and you will notice how he or she will try to attract as many people as possible. Most of the time of the opposite sex.
Assertiveness	As sweet and cosy as they can seem at times, when a Helper has decided that it is time his or her will should be done, a sudden rush of assertiveness comes into play. The Helper will push his or her will through no matter what the cost and keep on nagging till you give in.
Nurturance	The Helper is at his or her best when someone is in need. Especially in the case of ailments. When they can care for you, they deeply know that you must love them for it. Caring, the Helper is at his or her best.
False Abundance	Again their pride comes into play. Even when a Helper is as poor as a rat, he or she has to keep the image intact that everything is well. They'd rather buy you dinner than admit that financially all isn't going as well as things look.
Impressionable Emotionality	Helpers have strong emotional fits that seem to come out of the blue. All of a sudden a Helper can burst out in tears (it just happens to be in a private place, off course). Fortunately, it is as easy for a Helper to have these strong emotional outbursts as it is for them to feel good again.

Type III, the Successful Worker's Traits	My Short Description:
Attention Need and Vanity	Workers want to be in the spotlight. They want to be noticed. They spend a lot of time and energy thinking about what others would think of them. In order to make sure that everything looks all right they spend a lot of time on their looks.
Achieving Orientation	Success is everything. People will only notice and love you for what you have achieved. There is no place for losers.
Social Sophistication and Skill	But looks aren't everything: in order to look good, you have to know how to behave well too. Knowing what to do and say socially and do it with refinement and skill will ensure you of this in public's eye.
Cultivation of Sexual Attractiveness	Success in business or politics is great but it wouldn't be complete if you didn't achieve success with the opposite sex, too. Sex appeal remains important, no matter how high or oval your office might be.

Deceit and Image Manipulation	It's not so much that type III workers lie out straight (as type II Helpers tend to do, forced to do so by their pride). It's more that they are very creative with reality. Knowing very well that reality is what you make of it, the ability to put yourself and your work in a positive light is immensely valuable.
Other Directedness	What is success if there is no one to compliment you on it? Hence a strong affiliation to other people.
Pragmatism	"L'art pour l'art" sounds good, but if it doesn't wield any concrete results, type III workers will tend to shove it aside. Only things that have a strong probability of some decent return on investment gain the Successful Worker's attention.
Active Vigilance	Unlike the Perfectionist who has to have everything under control, the Successful Worker doesn't as much want to have things under control as he or she wants to know what's happening.
Superficiality	In the end only the bottom line matters. In the most superficial cases this really means just dollars.

Type IV, the Romantic's Traits	My Short Description:
Envy	They'll never admit it, these "romantic" types, but behind their façade they are bloody and cold materialists. If the neighbour has a more expensive car, they want one too. If a co-worker earns more money, they want it too. Try it with their jealousy for the other persons feelings and they'll agree with you.
Poor Self-Image	Romantics tend to have a poor self-image. Doubting whether they can do what is expected of them and whether they can make the right decisions.
Focus on Suffering	Romantics indulge themselves in their suffering. They kind of like the feel for it. "Oh, this is painful, I like it". They don't do this in the least to blame you for it, so that they can ask for amendments.
"Moving Toward"	Romantics are very much focused on other people. What do they think of me?
Nurturance	Romantics are great mothers, even if they are male. They tend to nurture their flock very well.
Emotionality	Passions run free in the Romantic. Not only can they become very sad easily (moving towards melancholia) but they are easily angered, too.

Competitive Arrogance	Romantics like fights, races and other matches. Especially emotional ones. When you get angry at a Romantic, he or she will respond by being twice as angry at you. "What, you are angry with me? Let me show you how angry I can be with you!"
Refinement	Romantics want love and attention but their strategy to get it is different than that of the type II, the Helper. Romantics want to be special. Refinement is one way of becoming more special than others.
Artistic Interests	In order to be special Romantics want to become a living work of art. Hence their romantic interest in the arts in general.
Strong Superego	Not such unrealistic perfectionism as with type I, the Perfectionist, but Romantics still have pretty strong ideals. For which they will fight hard too.

Type V, the Analist's Traits	My Short Description:
Retentiveness	Analysts want to keep their analyses to themselves.
Not Giving	On the same line they tend not to give to others what is theirs, i.e. their time and energy.

Pathological Detachment	Analysts fear to lose their personal freedom. In order to maintain their sense of freedom they detach themselves from material gains. They'd rather live with the bare minimum than feel they are being leveraged by a big salary, expensive car or in any other way.
Fear of Engulfment	The same goes for personal relationships. Analysts tend to keep people at a distance out of fear of being engulfed by the other and thereby losing oneself and his or her personal freedom.
Autonomy	Analysts are self-sufficient and have no problem being alone.
Feelinglessness	Both good and bad feelings are kept at a distance. It's pretty hard for analysts to feel feelings.
Postponement of Action	An analyst wants to feel safe by studying a subject fully before committing it to any action. Rather than actually do stuff, they will study it over and over again. There is always one more thing one can learn about a subject before action can be taken safely.
Cognitive Orientation	Knowledge is more important than feelings or action.
Sense of Emptiness	Having pushed their feelings away into the distance a sense of emptiness remains.
High Super-ego	Analysts have clear rules and ideals that should be followed, based on their own analysis.

Negativism	Any proper analysis of the current world situation moves the analyst towards negativism. This can be a sliding scale from irony to sarcasm and to full blown cynicism.
Hypersensitivity	I just love models full of paradoxes. Even with their feeling pushed aside, analysts are still hypersensitive. Any combination of the right or wrong words and the analyst is in tears. They tend to be rather emotionally withdrawn on the big issues but hypersensitive to the small things in life.

Type VI, the Loyalist's Traits	My Short Description:
Fear, Cowardice and Anxiety	Loyalists have a sixth sense for danger. They will look for the emergency exit whenever they enter a theatre. They will be too much of a coward to confront rowdy people. And more often than not they have all kinds of anxieties. Not in the least about their own physical health. Talk about hypochondria.
Over-alert Hyperintentionality	Loyalists tend to search for a hidden meaning behind everything you tell them. Even little unconscious gestures will be subject to close inspection to find the real message behind the imagined façade.

Theoretical Orientation	Fearful as the world is, the Loyalist likes to have a theoretical model of the situation. The better the model is the more grip a Loyalist has.
Ingratiating Friendliness	Loyalists are so friendly. Too bad the reason behind this friendliness is that they are scared. They'd rather have you as a friend than as an enemy. And having a lot of friends means you can travel in packs. So that when a real enemy appears you are not alone. Together we can win this fight.
Rigidity	Fixed behavioural patterns make for safe living.
Orientation to Authority and Ideals	Most of the time Loyalists have a clear picture in their mind of both the social and the career ladder. They will know what "upstairs" wants to hear and they will enforce rules and regulations "downstairs". But with a rebellious streak. They tend to make crude and agonizing comments on the management, but only when they can get away with it safely.
Accusation of Self and Others	First in line to point out who has failed where and when. Doesn't exclude him or her self though.
Doubt and Ambivalence	The problem for Loyalists is that they know that once you have committed yourself to some action it can go wrong. And that alone is dangerous in itself. Best to doubt as long as possible and check with others how they would handle things.

Type VII, the Hedonist's Traits	My Short Description:
Gluttony	Too much is always better than not enough.
Hedonistic Permissiveness	If it feels good it should be okay to do it or to continue doing it. When the neighbours start complaining about the loud noise at 4 am it is okay because we are having fun.
Rebelliousness	Any order must be overthrown.
Lack of Discipline	Discipline sounds like doing the same things over and over again. In other words: boring!
Imaginary Wish-Fulfillment	There is no need for actually achieving your desires. If you can imagine how it would feel if your wishes had been fulfilled this is more than enough to really enjoy yourself.
Seductively Pleasing	Hedonists don't like conflicts. So they will please you whenever they can. But they want you to join them in their hedonistic activities. So they'll start to seduce you to do more and more fun things.
Narcissism	In the end the only thing that counts is whether the Hedonist is having fun. Nothing else matters.

Persuasive	Hedonists can become very enthusiastic about their own ideas, no matter how grandiose they are. They are very capable of transferring this enthusiasm on to you. And they will persuade you to finance their enterprises and go along with things that on looking back would not have been very clever of you.
Fraudulence	Because the Hedonist knows from the start that his or her ideas are grandiose and not very realistic, the fact that they will infuse you with their enthusiasm for it anyway and sell you their ideas, means that in the end they will be fraudulent.

Type VIII, the Boss's Traits	My Short Description:
Lust	Lust for life. Lust for sex. It's important for Bosses to have a strong sense of being alive. This doesn't mean that you have to feel good. Pain can tell you are alive, too!
Punitiveness	For a type VIII Boss, the world is a smoking pit where every man must fight for himself. Think of Mad Max, if you have seen the movie. Bosses will enforce their own rules in their own environment and they will punish whoever breaks them.

Rebelliousness	Bosses are stubborn people and they will rebel against any authority that challenges their own worldview.
Dominance	You either eat or are eaten. Hence you need to dominate the scene or else bad things will happen to you.
Insensitivity	All that matters is that you get what you are after. Who cares about what other people feel while you grab what you can grab.
Conning and Cynicism	Hey, the good world died a long time ago. Nothing but dust and ashes remain. If you can get what you want by conning, hey man, go for it!
Exhibitionism	It's important to show who is boss in a group.
Autonomy	Bosses don't need anyone else to survive.
Sensory-motor dominance	Bosses are very physical. Their body is their fortress. If their body gets sick they feel betrayed and lost.

Type IX the Mediator's Traits	**My Short Description:**
Psychological Inertia	Mediators tend to postpone things. Not only in real life but also psychologically. They know they'll have to change, but, oh boy, changing is a lot of hard work and I am already getting tired at the thought of it.

Over-Adaptation	Mediators see the value of every proposition. This value-awareness tends to drive Mediators to over-adaptation. Rather than checking whether a certain opinion or plan fits into their own broader vision, they'll see the value of it and immediately feel the need to adapt.
Resignation	There is nothing you can do about it (without working up a sweat), so let's just leave it as it is.
Generosity	Mediators are always ready to help out. They are the true helpers of the Enneagram, rather than type II, the Helpers (who use it as a cry for attention and love).
Ordinariness	Mediators are prone to feel stress. What they want is peace of mind. Ordinary things bring peace of mind: a good job, a nice car, a relationship, a home etc. etc.
Robotic Habit-Boundedness	Life is easy if you don't have to think about it. Robot behaviour is the laziest way to live your life.
Distractibility	Ehhh, what was I doing? By seeing the value of every proposition, each proposition in itself is a distraction from the previous one.

Once again, this is just a rough sketch that you have to flesh out yourself by interacting with other people so that you learn what traits fit which Enneagram types. The more people you meet the better you will get at this.

THE ENNEAGRAM & PERSONALITY DISORDERS

f you look at the field of psychiatry today, you notice one thing in particular. They are moving away from classic psychotherapy and towards suppressive drug use. The famous Dutch Professor of Psychiatry von Danzig spoke well when he said: "Psychiatry is currently at the level that medicine was in the Middle Ages. We know what disorders exist, but we have no solution for any of them."

And this is true. I see many psychiatric patients that I get in my private NLP practise who have been in treatment for more than ten years. I look at the destruction of someone's personal life by these so called "psychiatric medicines." There is still a world to be won.

There is a logical explanation for this situation. After the colossal failure of classic psychotherapy, psychiatrists began to focus on scientifically measurable solutions. In other words: drugs. Not because these drugs solve mental problems very well, but because they do better statistically than classical psychotherapy.

Take the case of anti-depressants for instance. In scientific tests a 33% success rate is measured. Not something to be proud of. A disaster for someone like me who works with a "no cure no pay" philosophy. But a hell of a lot better than classical psychoanalysis which mountains of evidence suggest that it doesn't work at all. Together with a strong lobby of the medical-industrial complex, a lot of doctors are prescribing these drugs to people complaining of either anxiety or depression.

The problem is this. Our scientific knowledge is mostly about brain regions. Neurology today has a pretty good idea which function is performed by which part of the brain. But a mental problem isn't located as much in the brain itself, but at a much lower level, id est in the neuro-cortical pathways in the brain.

Whenever we learn something or experience something, our brain represents this knowledge by a neurological pattern called a neuro-cortical pathway. Basically this is a string of brain cells which are programmed to follow a particular path through the brain. Any behaviour is defined by the path the nerve signal travels after the initial trigger.

We still know almost nothing about what happens inside a brain cell. Why a brain cell transports information in a certain pattern rather than another. This is one of the reasons why our medical knowledge about the brain is so limited. We know something about larger brain parts, but we are still completely unclear about what happens inside a brain cell.

For instance, what any anti-depressant does is making sure that none of these pathways are travelled at speeds that make you feel very bad. By making sure that the brain is saturated with Serotonin (the neurotransmitter that keeps you calm and quiet), the drugs prevent any rash flowing of emotions. This lowers the anxiety experienced, but also flattens out all positive experiences. And, again, only for one in every three persons. The other two experience either no positive change at all or negative side effects.

The point is that the use of these drugs doesn't alter the neuro-cortical pathway. It just makes it harder for the brain to follow the path. Fortunately, the correct Neuro-Linguistic Programming and Neuro-Hypnotic Repatterning techniques as described in this booklet do allow you to make changes to the neuro-cortical pathways. By doing these exercises one trains one's brain to make it harder to feel bad. And at the same time to make it easier to feel good. Most people are very proficient at feeling bad but they suck at feeling good. The aim of NLP is to reverse this: to become an expert at feeling good and to fail miserably at feeling bad. But don't take my word for it, learn the skills involved and experience it yourself.

Most psychiatrists work with the DSM-IV classification. Unfortunately, the DSM-IV classification is linked too closely to the United States legal system to be of much value. It is better to work with the more neutral World Health Organisation (part of the United Nations) ICD-10 classification.

Now brace yourself and prepare for a good amount of negativity, because here comes the list of the ICD-10 disorders. I have included the official description just for completeness sake. I will comment on these immediately afterwards, so just read it to see what "the opposition" has construed.

F60.0 PARANOID PERSONALITY DISORDER

Personality disorder characterized by excessive sensitivity to setbacks, an unforgiving attitude towards insults; suspiciousness and a tendency to distort experience by misconstruing the neutral or friendly actions of others as hostile or contemptuous; recurrent suspicions, without justification, regarding the sexual fidelity of the spouse or sexual partner; and a combative and tenacious sense of personal rights. There may be excessive self-importance, and there is often excessive self-reference.

F60.1 SCHIZOID PERSONALITY DISORDER

Personality disorder characterized by withdrawal from affectionate, social and other contacts with preference for fantasy, solitary activities, and introspection. There is a limited capacity to express feelings and to experience pleasure.

F60.2 DISSOCIAL PERSONALITY DISORDER

Personality disorder characterized by disregard for social obligations, and callous unconcern for the feelings of others. There is gross disparity between behaviour and the prevailing social norms. Behaviour is not readily modifiable by adverse experience, including punishment. There is a low tolerance to frustration and a low threshold for discharge of aggression, including violence; there is a tendency to blame others or to offer plausible rationalizations for the behaviour bringing the patient into conflict with society.

F60.3 EMOTIONALLY UNSTABLE PERSONALITY DISORDER

Personality disorder characterized by a definite tendency to act impulsively and without consideration of the consequences; the mood is unpredictable and capricious. There is a liability to outbursts of emotion and an incapacity to control the behavioural explosions. There is a tendency to quarrelsome behaviour and to conflicts with others, especially when impulsive acts are thwarted or censored. Two types may be distinguished: the impulsive type, characterized predominantly by emotional instability and lack of impulse control, and the borderline type, characterized in addition by disturbances in self-image, aims, and internal preferences, by chronic feelings of emptiness, by intense and unstable interpersonal relationships, and by a tendency to self-destructive behaviour, including suicide gestures and attempts.

F60.4 HISTRIONIC PERSONALITY DISORDER

Personality disorder characterized by shallow and labile affectivity, self-dramatization, theatricality, exaggerated expression of emotions, suggestibility, egocentricity, self-indulgence, lack of consideration for others, easily hurt feelings, and continuous seeking for appreciation, excitement and attention.

F60.5 ANANKASTIC PERSONALITY DISORDER

Personality disorder characterized by feelings of doubt, perfectionism, excessive conscientiousness, checking and preoccupation with details, stubbornness, caution, and rigidity. There may be insistent and unwelcome thoughts or impulses that do not attain the severity of an obsessive-compulsive disorder.

F60.6 ANXIOUS [AVOIDANT] PERSONALITY DISORDER

Personality disorder characterized by feelings of tension and apprehension, insecurity and inferiority. There is a continuous yearning to be liked and accepted, a hypersensitivity to rejection and criticism with restricted personal attachments, and a tendency to avoid certain activities by habitual exaggeration of the potential dangers or risks in everyday situations.

F60.7 DEPENDENT PERSONALITY DISORDER

Personality disorder characterized by pervasive passive reliance on other people to make one's major and minor life decisions, great fear of abandonment, feelings of helplessness and incompetence, passive compliance with the wishes of elders and others, and a weak response to the demands of daily life. Lack of vigour may show itself in the intellectual or emotional spheres; there is often a tendency to transfer responsibility to others.

F60.3 is actually split up into *F60.30 Emotionally unstable personality disorder – Impulsive type* **and** *F60.31 Emotionally unstable personality disorder – Borderline type.* **Which brings the total to nine types of personality disorders.**

Now my hypothesis: that psychiatrists just found the nine Enneagram types of personality. Let me give some arguments for this hypothesis.

First of all it is good to realize that all this classification stuff is not real. It's only a model. And as such an abstraction away from reality. This goes for the ICD-10 classification and for the Enneagram. No one really has the F60.7 disorder. Nor is anyone really an Enneagram type seven.

But in order to process information about realities much faster we use models and abstractions. The justification for the use of a model lies in the practical effects its use can achieve. (This makes you wonder whether the practical effect of the use of the psychiatric models is nothing more than to hide the fact that they don't know what to do.

The personality disorders are just very sick versions of people's personalities. Or in terms of the Enneagram: the personality disorders are an unhealthy version of the Enneagram types. Or in other words: we all have a personality type. And depending on your personality type, if one thing or another has caused you to become an unhealthy version of your personality more and more, then you start to develop a personality disorder. It's a spectrum with on the one hand a healthy personality and on the other hand an unhealthy personality disorder.

But you can also turn this argument upside down. Behind every personality disorder is a healthy personality type. It is this personality type that has the potential to degenerate into a disorder but on the other hand it has a vital and healthy way of life. Yet the personality keeps the potential for the disorder. And this colours its characteristics. This is what makes us different from each other in case of a different personality. Or the same in the case of the same personality.

The Enneagram explains the personality traits as a survival method. After our birth there comes a time when, for the first time in our lives, we are left alone. During this time the infant realizes that he or she is not the same person as his or her mother. It is precisely at that moment that we choose or acquire a way to survive. And it is this way of surviving that creates our personality. The Enneagram postulates that there are basically nine survival patterns that one can follow.

This reeks too much of French Psychoanalysis for my taste and given Naranjo's background in psychiatry that may well be true. But given the ease at which you can see Enneagram types with very young children, aged three and up in some cases, it is obvious that the personality type is formed at a very young stage, if not at birth. On the other hand it's important to stress that the Enneagram types are not inherited from the parents or grandparents so a genetic basis would also be problematic. The metaphor that I use to explain how it works is that it looks as if it is some kind of configuration that gets selected very early on. Something that is very hard to change after the fact.

When I look at my clients' problems, I always see a positive intent behind their behaviour. This is one of the presuppositions NLP works with. The brain reacts on negative circumstances in the best way to ensure survival of the individual. Even if this means that the person in question suffers.

Take for instance a woman I worked with who had agoraphobia. In her case she was afraid to go far away (and a couple of miles was far away in her mind) because she felt that if something happened to her far away from her home, no one could rescue her, or they would be too late to do so. Furthermore she was experiencing panic attacks most of the time whenever she felt she couldn't "get away" either in a queue, in her car, on the road or in shops.

What happens (in my limited, but very practical model) is that her brain is registering a dangerous situation and is making sure that this is either avoided by use of a phobia, or that she gets out of the perceived dangerous situation as soon as possible by initiating a panic attack. All in good order to ensure the survival of the organism no matter what the cost to her life.

This links disorders and survival patterns. Or if you follow my suggestion that behind the personality disorder lies the personality itself, it links personality to survival. Exactly what the Enneagram presupposes.

In fact there is an entertaining story about how your Enneagram type is formed. When we are born, so the story goes, we are still a blank as far as our personality goes. Type zero, the Enneagram says. At the early stage of life we don't differentiate between ourselves and our mother. We are one big warm mass of (supposed) happiness where milk flows abundantly.

Until that one dark day, when you go shopping with your mother, and she forgets to take you back home. All alone in that unknown shop, you first realize that you are a separate being. Separated from your mother. And from safety. It is at this moment that you choose a survival mechanism in order to make sure that you survive. One of the nine available.

The first survival mechanism is Perfectionism. In order to survive you decide that only the highest standard is acceptable and that it is your role in the world to punish those who are found lacking. Surely, someone who works so hard for perfection; someone who tries so hard to make this world a better place; surely no one would dare attack such a person. In other words Perfectionism makes you feel safe. So you start tidying the shop and chastising those who make a mess of it, including the shop owner.

The second survival mechanism is Helping. Survival can only be guaranteed if you help other people. Why would anyone try to kill someone who is helping him or her? Safety is in Helping. So you start helping the shopkeeper and the customers. Carrying their bags, cleaning up the shelves. Whatever makes them love you and hence keep you safe.

The third survival mechanism is Success. Nobody in his right mind would kill someone like Einstein or Bill Gates. Or if they want to kill you, and you have enough money, you can buy safety. Basically the best strategy is to become as successful as possible. Only then you are safe. So you buy up all the milk in the shop and start selling it at a profit.

The fourth survival mechanism is Rareness. Imagine that you are a beautiful, unique and very rare living work of art. No one would dare damage such a treasure, would they? It's too important! So you change the way you look and act to create the image of a delicate piece of art. Surely everyone will see how special you are.

The fifth survival mechanism is Knowledge. Knowledge is power. If you know everything, you will also know how to survive. You will know how to control everyone. You will be completely safe. Hence you start studying the "How to run a shop" guide all alone in a dark corner where no one will see you while you are still on your way to gain all the knowledge you desperately need to ensure your personal safety .

The sixth survival mechanism is Fear. Fear everything. Doubt every action you might take, for it might be the wrong one. One wrong move can bring untold dangers to your doorstep. It's best to befriend everyone and ask them what they would do in such a desperate situation. So you start asking all the customers and the shopkeeper how they would handle things.

The seventh survival mechanism is Denial. Problems? No sir, no problem here at all. I am not even thinking about these problems now. Problems are the least of my problems. Couldn't be further away from my mind, these damn problems. And they sure don't pop up now and then. In fact I am just having fun, not caring about any problems at all. And so you turn the shop into a playhouse.

The eighth survival mechanism is Control. Hey, if you are the strongest, who is gonna hurt you? As long as you boss people around and get what you need, all is well. So you push the shopkeeper aside and start taking people's money.

The ninth survival mechanism is Mediation. What if there was no more war on the planet? If we all liked each other. Wouldn't that be great? Wouldn't that be *safe*? So you start helping to solve any dispute in the shop in order to create absolute harmony between everyone in the shop.

Did you recognize yourself yet? No need to hurry though, we still have many more insights to cover. Did you see some of the remarkable coincidences between the personality disorders and these survival mechanisms yet? Unfortunately the WHO doesn't follow the Enneagram type numbering (yet), but some are quite easy to spot.

F60.6 Anxious [avoidant] personality disorder **and the Fear survival mechanism are clearly the same so it seems.**

As soon as you realize that anankastic (Greek) just means perfectionist (Latin) the *F60.5 Anankastic personality disorder* **is easily linked to the Perfectionism survival trait. I would be the last person in the world to suggest that these psychiatrists are making up these difficult words only to hide the fact that they are clueless.**

F60.4 Histrionic personality disorder **basically means the hysterical person. The link comes when you realize that this is also the theatrical person. The one who thinks him or herself as a piece of art. Or in other words the Rareness survival mechanism.**

For the other links we need to delve a bit further into the Enneagram. First of all the *F60.0 Paranoid personality disorder.* **This one links to the Enneagram personality** type VII, the one using the Denial survival mechanism. Denial is quite social. All is well when you are in denial and all alone, but if there are others near they need to deny it too. Otherwise they might confront you or even challenge your denial. Lies are used to help the denial. Now you only have to watch out for those bad people that deny your denial.

F60.1 Schizoid personality disorder **links to the Knowledge survival mechanism. The Enneagram type V personality is living in his or her head so to say. He or she keeps people and emotions at a distance. Preferring the mind world. They want to know how the world works. They build this logical and understandable world in their head and then confuse this world with reality.**

The power of the Mediation survival mechanism is the ability to see the value of other people's viewpoint. In the Enneagram personality type IX this ability leads to dependency on others for well being. Hence it links with *F60.7 Dependent personality disorder*.

In case of the *F60.2 Dissocial personality disorder* **it's clear, too. Only the one who treasures success above anything else would murder to reach his or her goal. The end justifies the means. The success survival mechanism links with** *F60.2 Dissocial personality disorder*.

And finally the scourge of every therapist: *F60.3 Emotionally unstable personality disorder*, **or as they are known in the field: the Borderliners. Remember, this disorder is split into two subcategories: the impulsive type and the borderline type. The difference is basically that the former experiences bouts of aggression out of the blue (impulsive). And the latter bouts** of emotional tantrums (borderline), also out of the blue. This is exactly what happens with the Enneagram type VIII in case of aggression (control survival mechanism) and in Enneagram type II in case of emotions (helping survival mechanism).

To sum it up in an easy table of reference:

The Enneagram type	Personality Disorder
Type I, the Perfectionist	*F60.5 Anankastic personality disorder*
Type II, the Helper	*F60.31 Emotionally unstable personality disorder – Borderline type*
Type III, the Successful Worker	*F60.2 Dissocial personality disorder*
Type IV, The Romantic	*F60.4 Histrionic personality disorder*
Type V, The Analyst	*F60.1 Schizoid personality disorder*
Type VI, The Loyalist	*F60.6 Anxious [avoidant] personality disorder*
Type VII, The Hedonist	*F60.0 Paranoid personality disorder*
Type VIII, The Boss	*F60.30 Emotionally unstable personality disorder – Impulsive type*
Type IX, The Mediator	*F60.7 Dependent personality disorder*

Table 2. Mapping Enneagram Types **onto ICD-10**

When I first put this mapping together, I was astonished and amazed at what it implies. Now I am sure that you either feel the same (in case you have a lot of experience with the Enneagram) or you think that I just randomly linked and added stuff together without any justification.

Both reactions are correct. The Enneagram is a bunch of character traits randomly placed together to make nine different personalities. As far as I am concerned there is no logic behind it at all. And this is a good thing as you will see. Luckily for me I didn't invent the traits I gave each Enneagram type. They are readily available in any basic Enneagram book. If you don't know them, you can go and look them up. I am just pointing out that they do resemble the WHO ICD-10 personality disorders very well. Which gives me a clear indication that these are useful models. In fact I am convinced that sooner rather than later we'll have proof that these personalities based on survival mechanisms are pretty hardwired brain patterns. Both in genetics and in neuro-cortical pathways. Just like all the other behavioural patterns we work with in NLP.

Somehow many people come to me with different models as if I asked for them. If you have one, keep it for yourself and please don't bother me with it. I am more than satisfied with the Enneagram and see many faults with others. And each and every time I instantly notice one thing: all these models are logically sound. To me this is a clear indication that the model is also wrong.

Logic is a property of our ability for language. Or in different words: somewhere in our brain there are brain cells that provide us with the ability to reason. Those brain cells like logic. It makes them feel good. Illogical stuff makes them feel bad. Whether these brain cells feel good or bad has nothing to do with reality. In fact, reality is more complex than we can grasp with the part of our brain that has a preference for logic. If you want to feel this, go and try to explain quantum mechanics in words rather than in mathematics. After you have done this, do the same for a relationship. Soon you'll notice that reality is more complex than logic allows us to speak about it. Hence any logical model of reality must be wrong. An illogical model like the Enneagram is more in touch with reality. Especially if this illogic is proven by experience. To repeat: logic is a property of language, illogic is a property of reality.

It also works the other way around. Unrealistic statements presented in a logical fashion are easily swallowed by the brain as true and make you feel better. Try the following. Next time you feel not so good, tell yourself this: "I accept that I feel bad, but I remain calm and relaxed because I feel safe." You will notice a pleasant calm reaction to this statement, because your brain sees the syntactically correct structure and presumes it to be true. While in fact it is nonsense. How can you accept that you feel bad and at the same time remain calm and relaxed because you feel safe? I thought you felt bad. It makes no sense at all. Except to your brain it does. Just because the sentence has the word "because" in it, your brain accepts it as a cause and effect relationship. You see my point?

So for me it's a good indication of the model being in touch with reality when a model is illogical because it is based on experience rather than thought up by some theorist. The fact remains that logic is a property of our language. Not of the real world. Actually the real world is not logical at all. Again think about any love relationship you had that involved sex. Surely that relationship was anything but logical? Quantum mechanics shows us a world that makes perfect sense … in mathematics. Mathematically so complex that only a few people understand it. Mathematics that cannot analogically be explained in normal language.

Whenever I encounter illogical statements with regard to human beings they tend to be right. I'll give away a cheap but highly effective trick I use with my clients. Whenever one of my clients comes up with a logical cause and effect statement, I fervently deny it and turn it around. Cause becomes effect and effect becomes the cause. And most of the time I am right. This is due to the fact that with human beings almost all causes come from the unconscious and only then their effect enters the consciousness. But for the consciousness it seems that the effect has come first and it will assume that it is a cause since we all know that causes come before effects. Our conscious mind will then look for an effect and will find hints of the unconscious cause. Because it sees this after it has seen the effect the conscious mind will mistake the cause for the effect and vice versa.

For instance, if a client tells me (which happens way too many times) that he is feeling bad because his wife has left him, I tell him "no, your wife left you because you are feeling bad". And hey, I am right.

The same with the lady with agoraphobia I was telling you about and whom you might recall. She told me the following: "I got this problem (agoraphobia) after the death of my father. I had a bad time. I feared I would get depressed, but I didn't want that because I knew a few depressed people and well, they depressed me. So I got agoraphobia." What I hear is that she had a hard time surviving and that her brain was going for the depressive survival mechanism. But that, given her experiences with depressed people, she chose to get the phobia rather than a depression. Once I removed her traumatic experiences, it was safe again for her to let go of her phobia as it wasn't needed to prevent depression. Her story sounded as illogical as can be, so I guess it was right.

The same with the Enneagram. It's an illogical collection of character traits put into nine seemingly random categories. But wherever I look and whoever I test, they happen to fall precisely into one of these categories. Which for me doesn't add up to the reality of the model, as I know it's only a matter of abstraction. But it does add up to the usefulness of the Enneagram.

Let's pretend you are convinced. (While in fact you shouldn't be. First you have to finish the book and then go out and test this stuff first and follow your own experience by doing the techniques in the second half of this book.) This then leads to the question: "Ok, let's suppose you are right. What use is this model to us then?"

LEARNED BEHAVIOUR OR PERSONALITY?

S o what use is the Enneagram then? What's so handy about it that you use it even if it covers only a small part of everything you do? Well in order to explain this, I first have to tell another story.

In contrast to most psychiatrists I am quite happy with my success rate in helping people overcome their personal problems. (As I mentioned before: I work on a "no cure, no pay" base, so I need to be.) I am always intrigued however when I run into a brick wall with someone. Even though I concentrate on the things that go well, I always keep looking for ways to improve myself. And one way is to get early warnings signs of things that might not go as well as I expect. All as a result of life experiences such as this one:

The lady in question asked for my help with regard to fear of public speaking. This phobia was overpowering. Whenever she had meetings where she had to speak, she would be in such a terror that she simply refused to go. Her fear was that she would start crying in front of everybody like she had done on previous occasions.

For this problem she had seen psychiatrists and psychologists for the past then years which only made the problem worse. (They thought that exposure would improve her situation but it only improved her problem. By forcing her to cry before a group again and again, she ended up with not one trauma, but a whole series of traumatic experiences.)

Well, I started to teach her the correct NLP techniques to get rid of the trauma. To get her to feel good about herself. To dissolve the phobia. She reacted wonderfully. Felt great, her self-confidence built up again. She was ready to go to the next meeting feeling great. Unfortunately, there was no meeting at hand, so I couldn't test it immediately. But she had a meeting the following week and expected things to go fine. In short, no indication that anything was wrong.

Till the day of the meeting of course. About fifteen minutes before the meeting she called me. She was in her car on the parking lot of the meeting place. She had gone there, but out of the blue, all of a sudden she was struck with panic and emotions, and could not force herself to go inside.

I calmed her down on the phone, repeating the NLP practises. Everything worked fine. She hung up and we would call later that day to discuss this. Well to put it bluntly, it went badly. She got out of the car, walked to the front door, got another wave of emotions and went back home.

I did two more sessions with her. All the sessions went well as far as I can tell, but no results. After three sessions I told her I was sorry that I couldn't help her, that I would recommend someone else and that she of course didn't have to pay for my time.

She was an Enneagram type II, the Helper, or in the ICD-10 classification a Borderliner. (Nowadays I treat Borderliners in a different way but while my success rate has improved considerably it's still not as good as with the other types. Then again, Borderliners are notoriously difficult to help.)

That things can go quite differently shows the following case. This man was also a type II, Borderliner, but he had a somewhat different phobia. Or rather a collection of phobias. No problem at all with public speaking, but full-fledged agoraphobia and blood phobia. He was afraid to go to his hairdresser, let alone go to work.

When he was developing agoraphobia in his own home (as he described it; he started to be afraid of his own home), it was the straw that broke the camel's back. He downloaded a free guide I have on my site and called me the day after to make an appointment.

The first thing he told me at our first meeting was that based on the input from the free guide he was as good as cured. "Wow, how easy can this job be?" I thought. And in fact it was very easy. I showed him how he could do the stuff he had learned himself even better and to more effect. After having been home on leave for seven weeks with a burn out, he was back working full time again within two weeks, had a haircut and went on a holiday while we were still working together. Quite a different story, same personality.

Experiences like these led me to the conclusion that in some cases people were more easily detached from their problems than in other cases. Some people seem to cling to their problems while others part from them as if they throw away old clothes.

Whenever I looked at the differences between these situations, I noticed over and over again that problems tied up with someone's personality tend to be stickier than others. Sticky in the sense that they rather keep their personality and its accompanying behaviour than change. Rather than stopping the negative behaviour, it make more sense to teach them a more healthy variant of the same behaviour. On the other hand it appeared that problems not associated with people's personality tend to disappear more rapidly. This led me to the conclusion that there is a difference between whether a problem is alien and learned or a problem is a degenerated personality (disorder).

The former is much easier to get rid of than the latter. In fact treating them differently gives better results for both of them.

Hence it's important to know very early on in the process what personality someone has and which problems someone experiences and whether those two are linked or not.

For instance, one of my clients that I got in my private practise was depressed and experienced anxieties. The depression was over the unexpected death of his brother three years earlier and the anxieties were a fear of being fired. The Enneagram test showed that he was a type IX, Mediator. I immediately learned two things. First of all his depression did not fit his personality type and should be solved easily. Secondly his anxiety was a typical stress response for a type IX, Mediator.

And indeed it turned out exactly as I thought. After I taught him the right techniques as described later on in this book to stop the depressive feelings, he quickly overcame his depression. In fact on our second meeting he never mentioned the death of his brother and only talked about the job related stress.

For the stress related troubles I taught him the appropriate NLP techniques and showed him how he could become healthier within the Enneagram because the stress as anxiety response was so typical for him as a Mediator. This worked out wonderfully. Even though the company he worked for went belly up, he not only went through the whole ordeal relaxed and confident, but he also wound up as one of the five people who got their old jobs back when the company was bought up. Out of a hundred and fifty people originally working there.

I suspect that psychiatrists have noticed this too (I know nothing about that field but to talk them down, so excuse me if I state the obvious). They differentiate for instance between paranoia (F22.0) and paranoid personality disorder (F60.0) (God, I love these classification numbers. They look so cool. Can someone do the same for the field of NLP, please? I am sure we'll be much more scientifically respectable afterwards. Like really deep inside of us we want so badly ... not.)

What I do not know is whether they have come to the same conclusion as I have. People are an Enneagram type and have psychological problems at times. Sometimes these two are linked and sometimes not. Sometimes it is just ourselves becoming more and more unhealthy personalities, even resulting in personality disorders. And sometimes we can't help ourselves but learn, even if we learn some bad survival mechanism from somebody else.

Establishing whether someone has only learned some bad behaviour or whether it is part of his or her personality is important. It will guide you into two different directions. In case of learned behaviour it will be best if you unlearn the behaviour and replace it with more effective behaviour. In case of unhealthy personality traits you transform those into healthier ones. What I mean is that in my experience any personality trait has a negative and a positive version. And you are able to transform any negative one into a positive one.

Let me give you an example. I am a type III, successful worker. One of the traits of the successful worker is superficiality. In its on the negative side the trait makes a type III focus on money and sex.

But there is a positive variant as well. In the positive case, the type III is able to quickly leave bad events behind and it helps him or her to focus on the next day when everything will be beter again.

So if you find out which type your client is (which we will learn to do later on), then you can check to see what problems belong to him or her (so to speak). The Enneagram confounds things though by introducing the element of stress. The Enneagram is primarily a model for stress responders. When someone is stressed he or she "borrows" the negative character traits from another Enneagram type. If it ain't one of these then all other problems are learned behaviour. So there are basically three cases, namely:

1) The problem is unrelated to someone's personality. It's nothing more than badly learned behaviour.

2) The problem is stress which causes the client to borrow negative traits from another Enneagram type.

3) The problem is a personality disorder.

In my experience the first class of problems is easily solved with even the most rudimentary and basic NLP.

The second class of problems is also easily solved by teaching the client to stop stressing and start relaxing. Which can also be done easily with the proper NLP techniques and skills.

For the third and final class of problems I will list which approach is best to transform the unhealthy character traits into healthy ones.

So if you look at the different Enneagram types, here is a list of each Enneagram type and the associated problems:

The Enneagram type	Associated Problems
Type I, the Perfectionist	Obsessive/compulsive behaviour
Type II, the Helper	Anything with emotional fits (out of the blue) as is most common with Borderliners
Type III, the Successful Worker	psychopathic behaviour, "over my dead body" mentality.
Type IV, The Romantic	Hysterics, Theatrical
Type V, The Analyst	Schizophrenia
Type VI, The Loyalist	Fear
Type VII, The Hedonist	Paranoia
Type VIII, The Boss	Borderline where the person is aggressive (out of the blue)
Type IX, The Mediator	Dependency problems

We'll come back to stress related problems further on, for now we focus on the case where the problem is associated with the personality of the client. This requires a somewhat different approach. The following table briefly explains strategies and expectations that I use (nota bene, that means pay attention now in Latin, I only use the following list in case the personality matches the problem in the previous table.):

Type	Strategies
Type I, the Perfectionist	Pretty much following the standard NLP solution to obsessive/compulsive types. Give them a daily routine of happiness that they must follow. Expect a lot of criticism including that they will see treatment as a failure, but they are strong enough to continue their lives after all. These are grumpy people to begin with, so don't expect shiny happy faces any time soon. Make sure you use the feedback instead of failure pattern.
Type II, the Helper	Borderliner tough case. Expect a client who works wonders in sessions, only to report failure the day after. Emotions overtake the client and seem to come out of the blue. I focus on stopping these overwhelming emotions as fast as possible with anchors to powerful statements, positive memories and such. Build up the belief that with the same ease with which your client can be overwhelmed by negative emotions, he or she can feel good again.

Type III, the Successful Worker	I never seem to get these people in my practise, only their victims. Luckily I myself am a type III, so I know what's wrong with them. Overall NLP works wonders, but you might have to explain that your client should stop using "Operation Fridge" where he hides all his feelings in his personal refrigerator.
Type IV, The Romantic	Hysterics. Look-alike of the Borderliner in the sense that your client might experience overwhelming emotional fits out of the blue. But unlike the Borderliner the Romantic actually learns to stop these quite well. So expect no trouble here.
Type V, The Analyst	In case of schizoid problems the standard NLP approach of convincing the client to experience them in a positive way while keeping silent about his or her experiences to anyone who might think they are weird (which they are). It might prove pretty hard to get an Analyst to build up good strong feelings, as feelings on the whole are pretty far away from him or her anyway. This in the end turns out positively though; they can handle quite a lot. As long as they keep their weird experiences to themselves that is.
Type VI, The Loyalist	Standard NLP works wonders. The loyalist tends to be overly concerned with his physical health (hypochondria) and hence confuse physical reaction and emotions somewhat. (The difference between feeling fear and your heart beat going up.)

Type VII, The Hedonist	Once again NLP works wonders. They might take a while to get out of their heads to actually stop thinking before he or she starts to feel good and experience strong feelings. Client tends to have fantasies a bit too much, but once you have shown him or her that he or she can get bigger and better fantasies by paying some attention to you, you got him. Or her.
Type VIII, The Boss	The other Borderliner. The aggressive impulsive type. Actually, this one is even a bit harder to teach than the emotional type. He or she is pretty stubborn, thinks that only he or she is right. That his or her view of reality is the really real reality and that everyone else can drop dead for all he or she cares. In other words he or she might not be paying too much attention. NLP techniques work moderately well and even if they do, type VIII people tend to dismiss them the day after. Let alone use them for their own benefit. These are the people whom I expect hitting them in their face repeatedly might do them more good. (Nah, I am just kidding … ehhh not)

Type IX, The Mediator	NLP works very well, but there is one caveat. Mediators are what Naranjo calls psychologically lazy. After you have taught them how to stop their negative behaviour and feel good again, sometimes they just don't do it. Not because they can't but because they are too lazy to do it. They know they should change, but "oh man, what a lot of work that is". From the start I focus on teaching them discipline to actually make sure that they keep on doing the right things.

Now to simplify matters the nine Enneagram types are divided into three groups: the doers, the image people and the thinkers. Each type is either a doer, focused on image or a thinker depending on whether he or she can't cope with anger, feelings or fear. Basically, the image group is unable to handle emotions very well, the thinkers are unable to handle fear and the doers are unable to control anger all that much. Or to put it otherwise (Enneagram style): people behave the way they do, choose the survival mechanism they choose due to the fact that they are either unable to cope with their emotions, their anger or their fear.

Let's give you a table to show what this looks like:

The Enneagram type	*Personality Disorder*
THE IMAGE GROUP: CAN'T COPE WITH EMOTIONS	
Type II, the Helper Type III, the Successful Worker Type IV, The Romantic	*F60.31 Emotionally unstable personality disorder – Borderline type F60.2 Dissocial personality disorder F60.4 Histrionic personality disorder*
THE THINKERS: CAN'T COPE WITH FEARS	
Type V, The Analyst Type VI, The Loyalist Type VII, The Hedonist	*F60.1 Schizoid personality disorder F60.6 Anxious [avoidant] personality disorder F60.0 Paranoid personality disorder*
THE DOERS: CAN'T COPE WITH ANGER	
Type VIII, The Boss Type I, the Perfectionist Type IX, The Mediator	*F60.30 Emotionally unstable personality disorder – Impulsive type F60.5 Anankastic personality disorder F60.7 Dependent personality disorder*

And this kind of makes sense, because Borderliner – emotional type, hysterics and dissocial people certainly can't handle their emotions. Schizoid, anxious and paranoid people certainly can't handle their fears. And Borderliner – impulsive type, obsessive/compulsive types and dependent people can't handle their anger.

Now, once you know someone's Enneagram type, you also

immediately know what his or her primarly problem is. It's either fear, anger or emotions. Together with whether they are primarily doers, thinkers or image people. This is the first effective mind read.

For each type within a group, be it doers, thinkers or image people, there are three different ways of handling anger, fear and emotions respectively. One turns inside, one is outward, and the final one is neither in nor out.

In case of the anger types, type I, the Perfectionist, is the one that turns his or her anger inside. He or she will first get mad at him- or herself only to let the anger build up and up and only when it gets too much he or she will take it out on the surrounding people. Type VIII, the Boss is quite the opposite. He or she will never get angry at him- or herself, but only take it out on (innocent) bystanders. And finally type IX, the Mediator will neither be angry at him or herself, nor at the people he lives and works with except for the smallest outburst, which scares him or her as much as it does the surprised audience.

With the image people, we see that the type II, the Helper, hides his or her emotions and prefers to experience them alone. While type IV, the Romantic prefers a public display of emotions. Type III, the successful worker again is incapable of either showing emotions or going through them privately.

For the thinkers, the same holds true. Type V, the Analist, fears that people will invade his or her privacy and take away his or her freedom. While the type VII, Hedonist, fears are in the social forum: who's out to get him or her and challenge his or her denial. And finally type VI, the Loyalist, has neither these private or social fears, but just sees danger and risk all around, but decides not to let it have any impact[1].

Enneagram type	Focus	Result
THE DOERS GROUP, CAN'T COPE WITH ANGER		
Type VIII, the Boss	Outward	Only gets angry with others
Type IX, the Mediator	Neither	Can't get angry with him or herself, nor with others
Type I, the Perfectionist	Inward	Gets angry with him or herself first.
THE IMAGE PEOPLE, CAN'T COPE WITH EMOTIONS		
Type II, the Helper	Inward	Is emotional mostly in private
Type III, the Successful Worker	Neither	Copes with emotions by putting them in the freezer
Type IV, the Romantic	Outward	Social display of emotions

---

1   Traditionally this has been described as an anti-type, the so called anti-phobic Loyalist. But due to the above viewpoint I consider this the anti-phobic Loyalist the main type, and the phobic Loyalist the anti-type. See further on where I discuss anti-types.

THE THINKERS, CAN'T COPE WITH FEAR		
Type V, the Analist	Inward	Scared alone in fear of loss of freedom
Type VI, the Loyalist	Neither	Sees danger and risks but ignores them
Type VII, the Hedonist	Outward	Fears being exposed by others in social settings

What happens is this. The main function of the brain-stem inside our head is to recognize patterns that are an indication for danger. In case of danger our brain will produce stress hormones in order to protect the organism against the full effects of stress and the dangerous situation. Under the influence of stress people go into a survival mode. They will either do one of three things; they will flee, fight, or faint. The latter being a variant of the 'play dead' survival trick. The instinct to flee is generated by fear. The instinct to fight is generated by anger. And the instinct to faint is generated by depression annex emotions. Or to put it in other words, The anger types tend to fight, the thinkers tend to flee and the image people tend to get depressed.

This makes it easy to see whether a problem is learned, a stress responder or a personality problem. Anger with anger types is part of their personality. Emotional problems with emo types are also part of their personality as are anxiety problems with fear types. Later we will find out about types related typical stress responding behaviour. All other problems are learned. In my experience this is a large share of all problems I encounter.

Let me conclude with a repetition of the following remark: in most cases people have what I call "learned" problems. Their brain couldn't help itself and did what it does best: learn. And if the brain isn't learning good stuff, it will learn bad stuff. By taking a different approach for the cases in which a problem is more in line with a personality disorder, or as I would put it: unhealthy character development, you increase your overall success rate. This is done by introducing additional safeguards as explained in table 3.

VARIATIONS
BETWEEN
ENNEAGRAM TYPES

Many modern interpretations of the Enneagram come up with some way to change your Enneagram type. Either by "learning" positive traits from other types or by actually transforming yourself into another Enneagram type. This is a false picture. The whole point of the Enneagram is to be able to make distinctions between characters so that you can distinguish them. When you allow the possibility of acquiring character traits from various types, we all become little grey mice again and the model stops being useful. Within the

Enneagram, at some early development in your life, you make a decision for a certain survival-mode and your neurology seems to stick with that for the rest of your life.[1]

Each Enneagram type has a number of variations nevertheless. Additional detail is give by checking how healthy someone's character is, which Enneagram wing someone has and whether someone is stressed or relaxed. Besides these there are the so called anti-types.

To start with the health of a character. Enneagram types have positive and negative traits. When someone mainly displays negative traits he or she is said to be unhealthy. And the other way around: if someone embodies mostly positive traits, he or she is said to be healthy.

Reality is a bit more subtle than this. In fact each character trait can be either positive or negative depending on the circumstances and feelings of the subject as I mentioned before. For instance take again the shallowness so characteristic of the Type III Enneagram. In most cases this shallowness is a negative trait and any exhibition of this trait should suggest to you an unhealthy character. Yet in some situations it is better to avoid deep reflections and the shallowness becomes a sign of health. As a rule I find that by making use of any negative trait really, really well, you can transform it into a healthy positive version.

---

1 With the exception of Deep Trance Phenomena.

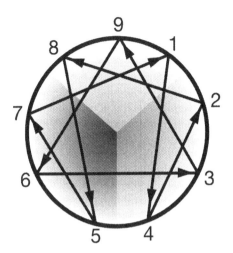

The second variation on the Enneagram is like zooming in onto each Enneagram type. By looking closer we see more details. And we notice that for each Enneagram type there are in fact two variants. In the picture of the Enneagram each type is positioned on the edge of a circle. People tend to lean towards one neighbour more than towards the other. This is called the Enneagram wing. So for each type you actually have two sub-types, one for each wing, colouring the character. I sum up these differences in the table below:

Enneagram type	Wing sub-types
Type I, The Perfectionist	- With type IX wing. A perfectionist with a lazy streak. Less inclined to work hard. Finds it more important to get a job, a wife, a house and a good car. - With type II wing. A perfectionist who is more sociable and willing to help. More emotional upheavals.

Type II, the Helper	- With type I wing. A helper who is more active, more perfectionistic and works harder. - With type III wing, A helper who is more entrepreneurial, more image conscious, less emotional.
Type III, the Successful Worker	- With type II wing. More sociable, more Inclined to help others and more emotional. - With type IV wing. More individualistic and more special
Type IV, the Romantic	- With type III wing. More entrepreneurial and more materialistic. - With type V wing. Very individualistic and more of a loner.
Type V, the Analist	- With type IV wing. More artistic, wants to be more special. - With type VI wing. More fearful and more focused on analysis and theoretical knowledge.
Type VI, the Loyalist	- With type V wing. More of a thinker, more theory and analysis. - With type VII wing. More of a bon-vivant, more sociable and busier with meetings and other social gatherings.
Type VII, the Hedonist	- With a type VI wing. More of a thinker, more risk aware and more analytic. - With a type VIII wing. More active, busier with doing stuff than just thinking about it.

Type VIII, the Boss	- With a type VII wing. More focused on personal enjoyment, very active and outgoing. - With a type IX wing. Quieter, more focused on gaining than on enjoying.
Type IX, the Mediator	- With a type VIII wing. More sexual, outspoken and more aggressive. - With a type I wing. More perfectionistic.

It's important to note again that even though an Enneagram looks somewhat like his or her wing type, they are in fact completely different. For instance some people find it hard to see the difference between a type VII with a type VIII wing and a type VIII with a type VII wing. Both are joyful, outgoing and active people. Nevertheless the differences are huge. The Hedonist tries to steer free from any conflict, whereas the Boss is actually looking for trouble. The Hedonist enjoys physical proximity and action, whereas the Boss gets irritated when people get too close, let alone when they start to push him or her. In such a case the Hedonist lights up, thinking that someone wants to play with him or her. The Boss, though, thinks that someone is challenging him or her to fight. Quite different I would say.

The third and most important variations are the stress and relaxation points. Each Enneagram type moves along the lines of the Enneagram sign in situations where he or she is under stress, or the opposite when he or she is relaxed.

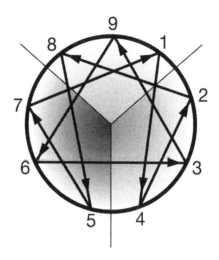

The reason this is most important is that as we have seen indications whether the mental problems they experience can be classified as learned behaviour, stress behaviour or personality traits. And the relaxation point indicates the type of activities the Enneagram type should engage in - to reduce stress and increase a strong feeling of well-being.

It's important to note the equivalence of the stress point with the negative traits and the relaxation point related with the positive traits. This equivalence is the following: in case of stress someone will exhibit the "borrowed" negative traits from the stress point, and at the same time whenever someone acts out these negative traits this will induce stress. Same with the positive traits and the relaxation point: whenever someone relaxes he or she will exhibit the positive traits borrowed from the relaxation point, and at the same time whenever one acts out these positive traits he or she will relax.

Make it absolutely clear to your client that it's pointless to remain acting on the stress traits. Not only isn't this behaviour part of yourself but continuing to do so will not get any result at all except for the continuation of stress. It is much smarter to simply stop the negative behaviour and start doing things associated with the personality or even better start to act on the positive traits from the relaxation point. If your client is unable to stop stressing right away use the appropriate NLP techniques to stop stress instead.

The following table sums up each stress point for each Enneagram type and the negative traits that are "borrowed".

Enneagram type	Stress point and related negative behaviour
Type I, the Perfectionist	Type IV is the stress point. Whenever a Perfectionist is under stress he or she will get very emotional and will start focusing more on what they want rather than what must be done. This is in fact a good thing because Type I has the inclination to forget what he or she wants by feeling too much that things just need to be done or must be done.
Type II, the Helper	Type VIII is the stress point. Whenever a Helper stresses he or she will get aggressive and in a foul mood and will start demanding that everyone does as he or she wants.

Type III, the Successful Worker	Type IX is the stress point. Whenever a Successful Worker stresses he or she tends to do one out of two things: either he or she starts doing all kinds of little things that are not important at all in order to refrain from doing what is necessary, or he or she will go into a passive mode not doing anything at all, paralysed by the stress.
Type IV, the Romantic	Stress point is type II the Helper. When a Romantic starts stressing he or she gets very emotional and starts whining to get attention.
Type V, the Analyst	Stress point is type VII the Hedonist. When stressing an Analyst flees into mindless partying and other social activities that are fun to do without facing the problem. He or she is running away from the real issue at hand.
Type VI, the Loyalist	Stress point is type III. Under stress the Loyalist starts focusing on money, becomes shallow and starts to hide his or her true self behind social masks.
Type VII, the Hedonist	Stress point is type I. The Hedonist, under stress, becomes very active and starts to make sure that all the little things are perfect but in a very foul mood and in a negative way.
Type VIII, the Boss	Stress point is type V. The Boss when stressing retreats to a lonely spot. He or she starts some senseless activity and doesn't want to be disturbed. Starts to ponder a lot without coming to any solution. Tries to learn and analyse what is wrong.

Type IX, the Mediator	Stress point is type VI. The Mediator starts to doubt a lot and becomes fearful. A lot of thinking going on. Focuses on theoretical knowledge.

If you spot these traits in your client, make sure you understand that stress is involved rather than the actual complaint. A good example was a Mediator that I worked with. When he came for his first session one of the first things he said was: "they say I have an anxiety disorder." My immediate reaction was: "but you don't experience it as such?" To which he answered: "No, not at all". And I said: "Well, then it probably isn't."

When we had done the Enneagram personality test it came out that he was a type IX, Mediator who happened to have a lot of stress in his life. When I asked him whether his negative feelings were rather stress related than anxiety related, he responded that indeed it appeared to him much more as stress than as anxiety. As soon as I taught him to relax rather than stress, his anxiety vanished without a trace.

For completeness sake here is a list of each relaxation point and its associated positive behaviour.

Enneagram type	Relaxation point and related positive behaviour
Type I, the Perfectionist	Type VII, the Hedonist is the relaxation point. Basically, Perfectionists start to relax when they enjoy and have fun. Go out more often.

Type II, the Helper	Type IV, the Romantic is the relaxation point. Walking in nature, going to the beach. Any interaction with mother nature relaxes Helpers.
Type III, the Successful Worker	Type VI, the Loyalist is the relaxation point. Sitting back, thinking things over and becoming a little more risk aware and the type III will relax more.
Type IV, the Romantic	Type I, the Perfectionist is the relaxation point. Working hard and doing your utmost best at your work, really relaxes the Romantic.
Type V, the Analyst	Type VIII, the Boss is the relaxation point. Action time. Taking the lead and starting to do stuff relaxes the Analyst. After all, he or she got it all figured out by now.
Type VI, the Loyalist	Type IX, the Mediator is the relaxation point. Starting to act and helping others will relax the Loyalist.
Type VII, the Hedonist	Type V, the Analyst is the relaxation point. Just retiring and being alone for a while and reading or writing a good book. This will relax the Hedonist.
Type VIII, the Boss	Type II, the Helper is the relaxation point. Ironical as it may be, the Boss finds relaxation once he starts to help others.
Type IX, the Mediator	Type III, the Successful Worker is the relaxation point. Starting new projects. Taking initiative. Thinking about practical bottom line results. That will relax a Mediator.

The final variation is the anti-type. Also known in NLP as the polarity responder. Best known in Enneagram literature is the anti-phobic type VI, Loyalist. This is the most obvious one. This type would be a Loyalist who would answer negatively to any question regarding their fear and anxiety. What happens is that they actually do see the danger, but immediately act as a polarity responder. They will tell themselves that if they let their lives be influenced by the fear and anxiety they feel, they will end up nowhere. So they'll conjure up a lot of courage and will act anyway. (Not the best strategy. Courage takes a lot of energy. Acting from strength is much easier.)

In my years of experience, I have reached the conclusion that each type has its anti-type. Most of them are much more subtle than the anti-phobic type VI, Loyalist. What happens is that they will respond differently to the test questions. Nor will they recognize themselves in each trait in the list later on. But as soon as you suspect they may be an anti-type, check to see whether they are simply denying or countering the question or trait but that it is an issue in their life nonetheless. The difference is that instead of having a direct influence on their lives, it has an indirect influence, namely by acting out the denial. Most of them will agree that it is an issue but that they either simply deny it our counter it. Here is a list of the anti-types:

Enneagram type	Anti-type
Type I, the Perfectionist	In principle opposing all principles. Angry against anger.

Type II, the Helper	Wants love and attention by obviously not helping where help is needed most.
Type III, the Successful Worker	Creates the image of the most successful loser.
Type IV, the Romantic	Wants to be so common that it becomes extraordinary.
Type V, the Analyst	Has come to the conclusion that analyses are worthless
Type VI, the Loyalist	Increases courage to overcome anxiety
Type VII, the Hedonist	Rather than not tell anything about myself, I will tell the whole world everything about myself (but not my true self).
Type VIII, the Boss	It's my rule that I don't rule.
Type IX, the Mediator	Full of disciplined outer action to mask the lack of psychological change.

CONVICTIONS CONVICT AND HOW ABOUT NLP?

Wow, what an enormous list of limiting beliefs, convictions and presuppositions. No wonder most NLP practitioners stay away from the Enneagram. Couldn't it be that by working with the Enneagram model, you tend to limit yourself and as it were create a self-fulfilling prophecy?

That this is not the case is of course hard for me to argue. Not only did I work with the Enneagram before encountering NLP but I also found it most valuable. So it could very well be that if someone else had been in my shoes he or she would have solved the unhealthy character cases easily and without any problems. No doubt someone with more experience and skill would have gotten better results.

Yet, I am all in favour of rigorous testing. And although hardly scientific, I have done many experiments. In one I would treat a client without any use of or reference to the Enneagram. In the cases I didn't use the Enneagram, at the end of the treatment, I would list for myself what kind of problem that specific client had, note whether I was successful or not and only then establish the Enneagram type at the end of the last session. Other experiments would be the other way around. I would start establishing the Enneagram type and find out whether their problem was related or not. Then I would adapt my strategy accordingly.

Having done this for more than a year I found out that the success rate was higher in the group I used the Enneagram model with than in the other group. I also found out that in the cases of group one where I didn't use the Enneagram approach the least successful cases were the ones where there was a link between the problem and the client's character.

Currently, I keep the distinction between "personality" problems and "learned" problems at the back of my mind. But one thing kept bothering me: what to make of this concept of character or personality?

This brings me to one of my favourite topics which most authors writing about the Enneagram simply ignore or get totally wrong.

The Enneagram types, and hence someone's personality, is not about the substance of man, but about form. Let me explain.

What you do and who you are – who are you – that's very substantial, so I consider it of substance. It's the content of your life so to speak. This has nothing to do with how you do things. Your personal style - how you accomplish things - I call form. This is your character or personality. Someone could do the same things that I do but have a completely different personality. But when someone behaves in the same way I do, even if he does completely different things, you could say our characters are alike.

I for once, had a lot of sympathy with all the creative book keeping that seemed to be going on around the turn of the century. In my view each and every Enneagram type would make a great accountant. And a bad one too for that matter. Only the style in which they would do their accounting differs. Perfectionists will go for excellent records, Successful workers will go for any opportunity to squeeze out some more profits and Hedonist accountants will be very creative. The good ones would of course not cross the line of legality like the bad ones do.

This is an important distinction because it clears away almost all of the paradoxes between the Enneagram and NLP. NLP is about both substance and form, i.e. technique and attitude. But even with the same attitude you can have many different styles. The Enneagram is only about form. So even within the model of the Enneagram you are absolutely free to become whoever you want to be. The only limitation the Enneagram model brings to the surface is that you are somehow stuck with the style in which you do things. (As opposed to the more common idea of how you do things technically in NLP.)

But it is precisely this choice in style, in how we do things, that creates our personality. When this style develops in a negative or unhealthy way we get problems that require a different approach or strategy. Working with the Enneagram gives you ideas ......about the direction you should take to gain a healthier style. Transforming unhealthy habits into healthier ones.

Let me give a few examples to make things clearer. For instance all nine character types can be artistic (substance) but the style or form through which they would express themselves would be an expression of their personality. All nine types could be great salesmen (substance) but their style (form) would be different depending on their character.

The archetypal artistic type in the Enneagram is type IV, the Romantic. But in real life you would find that any Enneagram type can be a great artist. Gustav Klimt for instance makes typical type IV Romantic art, whereas Mondriaan has more of a type V, Analytic style. The same goes for salesmen. A skewered account of the Enneagram often suggests that type III, the Successful Worker would be ideal for the job of salesman. But this is wrong. Every personality type would be able to perform equally well. They would only differ in the style they use.

In fact, most people wouldn't view their personality as a limitation as some NLP trainers would suggest, but would be proud of it. Character is what colours their lives. It is the flavour that makes this journey on earth worthwhile. Without personality we would all be the same. So it is precisely to safeguard this precious gem that I use the Enneagram to stop unhealthy consequences and make life healthier.

And that is exactly the beauty of the Enneagram. I began my story with the revelation when I thoroughly understood that other people are really different from me. From this understanding grew respect and admiration for the otherness of other people. I no longer think them stupid. On the contrary they have become strangely interesting. The nine Enneagram types aren't nine cages in which we force people. If you look at the Enneagram sign and take that for everything there is, you will notice something.

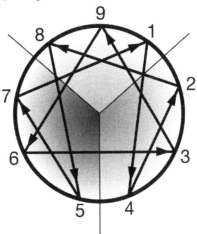

If we look at it from a bird's eye perspective we see everything in a symmetrical way. But imagine yourself standing on one of the nine points (preferably your own) looking out over a big field with the Enneagram sign on it. From each perspective you will have a completely different picture, a completely different viewpoint. This is what makes one Enneagram type radically different than the other eight types: it has a unique perspective of the world. Without any way to see the other person's perspective there is a wide gap between the deep understanding of ourselves and our knowledge of others.

To overcome or limit this gap, the best strategy is simply to go out, meet people, establish their Enneagram type and open your eyes and ears and learn how they behave. Compare them to other people of the same type that you have met before. See what they do the same, see what they do differently. Keep it limited to the style they use, the way they do things, the manner in which their personality colours their actions. Not everything you'll see them doing or hear them saying ties in with the Enneagram. A lot of stuff simply has nothing to do with it. People tend to come up to me with the strangest questions asking whether this and that is an indication for a specific Enneagram type. The answer most of the time is just "no." Only traits that you observe with many people of an Enneagram type are part of the model.

I am in the wonderful position that hundreds of people come to see me each year. And while they come to learn from me, in fact I learn even more from them. One of the most eye-opening workshop activities you can do with the Enneagram is to place all participants of one type on stage and start asking them questions about how to do things like them.

When I first experienced this I was amazed how it was possible that the guy next to me gave the answers that were inside my head. How did he know that? My lovely girlfriend happens to be the same type as I am (Type III, the Successful Worker) and I am regularly amazed every time she is thinking my thoughts.

But there is a flipside to every situation. While it is amazing how perfectly well you can understand your own type, it is still very hard for me to understand all the eight other types. Even though I am supposed to teach other people these types, I see myself more as grasping the other personality types intellectually, rather than with full understanding. The real experts (well, except for my own type III) are the people who visit my workshops. I am just very capable of getting their personality traits on display. (By the way, in the end this is a good thing. I wouldn't want to miss the mystique of the unknown for all the gold in the world.)

In all my years of study I have experienced only one possible way into the realm of the other personalities: Deep Trance Identification. One of the well known deep trance phenomena is Deep Trance Identification with which you convince someone that he actually is someone else.

Always fun to watch on stage, but it happens to be useful whenever you want to integrate your knowledge about someone more deeply. Deep Trance Identification allows you to experience what your brain thinks what is to be like someone else.

When I underwent Deep Trance Identification for the first time, I found it a wonderful experience. One that enlightened me on a subject I had studied for many years in totally new and unexpected ways. Less intellectual and more integrated and from a "touchy feely" point of view if I make any sense at all.

I am pretty sure that you could use this technique to come closer to the other view points (even if you would never know for real whether that was really what it was like). I happily invite any capable hypnotist to come and visit me for a series of experiments to see how close we'll come.

So in the end NLP wins in deciding whether we can change everything and everyone, or whether you stay the same character all your life. But I hope that in the struggle to get there, you have found the Enneagram to be too valuable a gem to throw away. And given the fact that most people rather prefer to remain themselves than to stay in deep trance (there are some exceptions, yes I know) it's better to know how to stop unhealthy consequences of character and to become a healthier version of yourself.

HOW TO USE THE ENNEAGRAM IN CHANGE WORK

The Enneagram is especially useful in Change Work, i.e. any work you do where the objective is to change someone's feelings, convictions and behaviour. Once you have established what someone's Enneagram type is, you know immediately what the best way is to engage him or her. And you know which problems are associated with the personality, which ones are stress related and which ones are learned bad behaviour. On top of that I use the Enneagram to mind-read someone fast to build convincer states.

Convincer states are special states where you convince the client that change is about to happen, their view on their own limitation is limited indeed and that, even though they had a hard time believing, they can overcome the problems they had. When seemingly out of thin air you describe their most private motivations and feelings, you convince them that indeed they have come to the right person for a change.

With any Change Work, the first thing I do is decide whether I will use the Enneagram openly or covertly. This depends more on the flow of things than on anything else. If I am hitting it off with the client immediately and we get into NLP quickly, I don't interrupt the flow just to find out about the Enneagram.

This can be easily done by not formally asking the questions, but by checking whether the problems the client recounts are linked to any of the Enneagram type questions. To give an obvious example, if a client talks about long periods of emotional depression coming out of nowhere, I throw in a question here and there about whether they like to help people and if you expect something in return whenever you help someone. As you can see I check for any links between the presented problem and any potential personality disorder like Borderline – emotional type in this instance.

Another obvious example is to check whether people who fear one thing or another also doubt a lot (checking for type VI, the Loyalist). Or another example: at some point a client of mine complained about anxiety. I had already gotten a few signals that he might very well be a type IX, Mediator. In order to check whether he really was a type IX, Mediator who was just stressed out, I ask him whether peace of mind is important to him. He reacted immediately and very intense. Peace of mind was one of the most important things for him. Once you start using this you will notice that the more you get acquainted with the model, the better you get at checking covertly.

In any case where I either feel that we need to jumpstart the meeting or where the client's problems aren't exactly clear, I start with the Enneagram openly and formally. The way I introduce the Enneagram is by taking it to extremes to inoculate any negative feelings about labelling and framing. I explain that the Enneagram is a way to put six billion people in nine little cages and never let them out again. But then I'll go on explaining that it's only a model about how we do things, not about who you are. And that I won't use it except to quickly look for any pitfalls someone may have in their character.

I continue to explain that the test consists of a number of questions, but that it isn't an intelligence test, nor a quiz where you can win prizes. I stress that any answer they want to give is the right one, as is any reaction. There are no wrong answers in this test. Finally I ask them whether they are okay with it and if we can start. From there I start with the questions from the previous section.

Once we have established the Enneagram, I figure out whether their behaviour is learned or character-related. In the former case

I'll act relieved and tell the client that it's ok because it's just learned behaviour and that it's something foreign to them and that the only thing that needs to be done now is to learn new and more effective ways of behaviour.

If it's the case of a personality related problem, I explain that it's in their nature to have this kind of problem, but that I have met a lot of people who had the same problem but who were perfectly capable of learning better and more effective ways of dealing with these issues. In fact they can become so good at it that it becomes a strength rather than a weakness. Furthermore, that the purpose of the treatment is to make sure that the client will be able to stop the negative behaviour as fast as possible and recover from it quickly so he or she can continue to start feeling good, even if the problem doesn't disappear completely.

For me this is the best way to frame it. Because either way the result is that the problem disappears completely and that they'll live a happy and fruitful life. Or they are capable of stopping any negative feeling in the bud and start to feel good again for no reason at all. What is most important is that they are, once again, able to steer their lives into a better and healthier direction where they can enjoy the moments of life more and more than they used to.

In order to build convincer states for the client, I shortly tell the client about the most common traits for the Enneagram type. It's a good way to create an atmosphere of wonder and impress the client with a subtle way of your expertise as you start telling him or her "deep insights" into his or her character. Of course, many times they themselves have told you about those traits in the test.

It's important to realize that sometimes your client is checking you out. With the Enneagram you are able to mind-read your client fast and give him or her verifiable information about himself or herself. Deep insights that seemingly unexplainable come to mind. This communicates not only your expertise in these matters but also that amazing things that the client thought to be impossible suddenly seem to become possible. Another big stride into the right direction. You open the door again to the magic reality once had when they were a little child. Anything becomes possible, in their minds. Change seems easier and closer by than they used to imagine.

The best way to explain an Enneagram type to someone is to remember someone you know well. Go back and remember how they acted. What was typical for them and what not. I have a number of friends, relatives and other noteworthy characters that I can conjure up to explain specific character traits.

Finally, it is good to tell your client about the stress and relax behaviour. These are two way streets. That is to say: whenever someone stresses he or she will display the stress behaviour. But when he or she is acting out the stress behaviour, stress will follow too. Also in the case of relaxation. Whenever your client relaxes he or she will display the relax behaviour. But even more important: whenever your client starts to act out the relax behaviour, relaxation will follow.

So it's important for your clients to recognize their own stress behaviour. After all they are the ones who get the tell-tale signs that they are actually stressing. Now to stop the stress, they'll just have to change their behaviour from stress behaviour into relax behaviour and relaxation will follow. Learning to recognise stress related behaviour as a sign of stress and knowing how to cope with stress through NLP ensures that they will be able to steer themselves in the right direction quickly.

As you see I myself use the Enneagram as some kind of diagnosis tool. Now it is important to explain that I don't believe in diagnosis nor am I qualified to give one. Hence I will always keep this to myself and never tell the client whether he or she has X or Y. I think that most psychiatrists use diagnosis to hide the fact that they don't know what to do.

On the other hand I use diagnosis to remind myself what to do or refrain from. My diagnosis is twofold. First there is the personality disorder and then there is the problem reported by the client. For instance a Borderline impulsive type personality disorder with a fear of public speaking. Or a schizoid personality disorder with depression. Or an anakastic personality disorder with obsessive/compulsive behaviour.

Once again, I check whether there is a link between the personality and the reported problem. If that is the case I make a mental note to explain the client's inclination. If not, I plan to check for the associated problem with the personality disorder. Whenever a client experiences a different problem from what you would expect given his or her Enneagram type, I get very curious as to how they deal or have dealt with the "expected" problem.

Most of the time you either hear that it was a problem but that they got over it somehow (and I then use the way they got over it to help them get over their current problems), or it turns out that they use a different description of the associated problem than the one I use. It is not uncommon for people to find it pretty hard to distinguish between insecurity, depression and fear. There is a reason that general practitioners prescribe anti-depressants to people with anxiety problems. Most of the time the problem is quite vague and people can use a lot of different terms to explain things. Or they might feel ashamed about their problems (which is a good indication that you are dealing with the "I can't cope with emotions" group).

So in the end I use the Enneagram more as a reminder for myself to check with previous similar cases I have known to be sure I am taking the best approach I know or to improve upon myself where I previously made mistakes.

HOW YOUR
BRAIN WORKS
(ACCORDING TO NLP)

My main beef with the Enneagram isn't as much that it is too limiting or full of negative presuppositions. But I am bothered by the fact that after having established correctly what is wrong, it doesn't offer concrete steps how to correct it. It's very much like dr. Phil, the well-known TV personality. It's one thing to know what's wrong and to tell clients that they should change their behaviour but if you can't tell them how, you won't accomplish very much.

That's the reason NLP is my first and only love. With NLP you not only find great ways of collecting information but also get clear handles on how to take care of a variety of problems. With NLP you gain a good grasp on what should be done in varying situations. Now, there are many NLP books describing this. Unfortunately, most of them just repeat techniques which I consider ancient (in fact they are just twenty to thirty years old). What you don't get from these basic guides is the skills to make change work gracefully.

One of the things lacking is a clear picture of how the brain works. Without it you don't understand what you are dealing with. Some basic neurology is necessary in order to understand what the effect is of the NLP techniques you practise.

First of all the brain is a biological information processing system. The information coming into the system is sensory information. We see, hear, feel, smell and taste. There is no other source of information about the outside world than through the five senses. This means that everything the brain does is coded in sensory data. Whether we remember something, fear something or experience pleasure, it all happens due to sensory data being processed in our brain.

All sensory data flows from the senses to the brain. The brain-stem to be precise. This oldest part of our brain (it can be found in ancient reptiles) processes this information by adding layers of higher abstraction on to it. The raw experiential data is transformed into more and more complex objects. These objects are thereafter scanned by the brainstem to see if they match any known danger pattern. If not, the highly abstracted experiences are routed to our neo-cortex where our consciousness is found and we experience reality as we know it. This whole process takes about one second. One of the reasons you should always stay at least two seconds behind the next car is that you will not see the driver in front of you braking if you are closer than one second.

If the brainstem finds a match to a known danger pattern it doesn't route the experience to the neo-cortex directly, but rather sends it to the lymphoid system where our emotions reside, because the lymphoid system is much faster to react than our consciousness. It will induce stress and force your emotional system to cope with it and to do whatever it has learned to do in such a situation.

This was a good thing a couple of thousands of years ago when we were going hunting in the jungle. If we ran into a bear we should either run away fast or start fighting immediately. Not start thinking the encounter over. If the moment a bear appears you start to evaluate between the advantage on the one hand (bear steak tonight, a nice bear hide in front of the fireplace in your cave) and the disadvantages (strong claws, sharp teeth) on the other and then start calculating the best strategy to kill the bear (just hit him at the right angle on his head with your baseball bat), you are basically way too slow. You would have been eaten a long time ago. So maybe humanoids who reacted this way might have walked on the face of the earth some time, but they all got eaten. Our great- great- great grandfather though just reacted emotionally. That is to say, fast.

What happens when you react emotionally is that the lymphoid system takes over. The stress of the danger produces three typical survival patterns:

- Danger produces stress which induces fear so you run away.

- Danger produces stress which induces anger so you start to fight.

- Danger produces stress which induces depression so you give up, roll over and play dead.

These are of course the three basic reactions as predicted by the Enneagram model. To sum up: perceived danger produces stress which induces either fear, anger or depression.

In order to make sure that the biosystem works as fast as possible the emotional center starts to send fake and misleading information to the neo-cortex to keep our consciousness busy and out of the loop. We all experience this when we get angry. All of a sudden you lose control and start yelling things you really didn't want to say, and you can't think clearly. Two hours later when all the emotions have subdued you suddenly come up with all these really great rational things you should have said, but were unable to think of during the fight.

Worse yet, we don't even need perceived danger from outside. Our brain is capable of adding sensory data to our raw experience. Just look to your left now and remember what your bike, car or living room looks like. All of a sudden it is as if remembered images are superimposed in your visual data stream and you can "see" what you remember these things look like. Now mark the word see. It's not the same quality of pictures that you see normally. Our brain doesn't have an internal graphic card that can generate the same amount of visual information data that our eyes can. But the information is there.

Now the problem is that this sensory information that your brain creates (you can do this for all five senses by the way. Some people are just more used to one than the other) is put into the raw experience stream that is being analysed by your brainstem. And your brainstem is unable to notice the difference between information our senses get from the outside world and information that our brain produces itself. In other words: remembering what a bear looks like, feels like, sounds like, tastes like or smells like, produces the same effects on our brainstem as a real bear. If the brainstem has a danger pattern for bears, that pattern will be triggered. The emotional reaction will follow even if you know rationally that it is nonsense. We just can't help ourselves.

Take fears for instance. Some people make the distinction between real fears and unreal fears. This is wrong. For the person experiencing the fear it is real. That's the problem. A better distinction would be between useful fears and non-useful fears. Some fears are good to have since they protect you from bad things happening to you. But for all other fears it's better to stop them as they have no use any longer.

Talking about abstractions, it's important to note that the problem is not the way our brain has all these different centres that do all kinds of different work, but that the real problem lies with the pathways between different parts of our brain.

A brain cell has about the same computing power as a PC. Except that it also has about 300.000 thousands ways to connect with other brain cells. Behaviour is caused by information travelling a specific path through the brain. This is a strong "is". The "is" of identity (A really is B): whenever that path is travelled the behaviour (I count feeling as a specific behaviour) follows. So when you want to help people change negative and limiting behaviour, you have to use techniques that actually break up the old pathway and create a new one.

If not, you get the situation where each time people behave in a certain way, the brain and specifically the involved brain cells are trained more and more to follow this specific path. Not only that, due to the biological nature of the brain, neighbouring brain cells will soon start to follow the negative patterns, thus reinforcing them.

That's one reason why anti-depressants work so badly. They act on the level of the whole brain by making sure that information travels less forcefully through the brain. This causes the negative behaviour and feelings to have less impact, but the same goes for all the positive feelings and behaviour patterns. The real problem at the level of the neuro-cortical pathways is not dealt with. One of the reasons that people quitting anti-depressants fall back into their old habits. The same is true for bad therapy.

What is needed is a way to break up the old pathways and create new ones. Preferably in such a way that the brain cells involved in the negative behaviour are used in the new and more positive pathway so that they will be unable to remember how to pass the information along the negative pathway (I know that some brain cells are involved in our memory, but at the same time brain cells themselves learn and remember where to send certain information to. Scientific knowledge about our brain is still very limited but even less so about what is happening information wise in our brain cells).

Luckily, we can use the same process that creates stress and the survival reactions of anger, fear and depression to create good feelings instead. The same way our brain-stem triggers unhappy feelings and emotions, it can also trigger good feelings. Now I know there has been a time when you felt really really good. I don't know where or when it was, but I do know that when you remember a specific moment in time you can see where you were and with whom you were there.

As soon as you remember what the place looked liked, check whether you see yourself in that picture or image. If so, the image you remember is constructed by your mind, as you have never seen this in reality. When this occurs make sure you float into your body so that you see what you saw, hear what you heard and feel what you felt.

If you are remembering a pleasant time or a moment of happiness, I am sure that it feels good to think about it. If you don't notice these feelings make sure that you contrast them with a memory of something bad. I know that you would rather think back to pleasant times than to bad times. Just notice the difference. Somehow your brain has to be able to make a distinction between good and bad memories. Your brain does this by having one feel different from another. That's why thinking back to times when and places where you had a lot of fun feels better than otherwise.

As you see, you can use the way your brain works in your favour. By forgetting the bad times and remembering to focus on the good times, you actively change your brain chemistry and start to feel good. For some people, especially when they have been hit by hard times, this seems easier said than done. Due to the bad habit of feeling bad it has become quite difficult to feel good. In these cases you need specific techniques to confuse the brain cells involved in the negative behaviour or feelings so that they unlearn how to send information on the wrong neuro-cortical pathway. If, after you have confused your brain cells enough, they will start to learn and pick up any pattern that makes you feel good. That way you become worse in feeling bad and become better at feeling good.

NLP, as taught today nowadays by dr. Richard Bandler, has developed three rapid techniques to confuse brain cells. What these techniques amount to is to change the information processed by the brainstem, that is the sensory data. Because feeling, hearing and seeing are the major senses that most people are conscious of, the techniques focus on these three senses.

STOP FEELING BAD AND START FEELING GOOD

The most important technique is the one to get more grip on your emotions. Unlike popular belief you exert a lot of control over your emotions. By using the following technique you stop bad feelings and start to feel good again for no reason at all. Do it correctly and your brain unlearns the bad behaviour and associated feelings and learns more and more to feel good in such a way that it becomes automated unconscious behaviour. The effect is that you will find it very difficult to feel bad and very easy to feel good.

In my case for instance, even if my clients tell the most horrible story, I would have to really try to feel bad about it. In fact I keep feeling good and keep smiling because empathizing with their bad feelings would only make matters worse. At one time a young Moroccan woman came to see me because she had a history of twenty years of mental and physical abuse by her mother (she didn't want to be wedded to her nephew). She had severe trauma and she was a type II, Helper so her borderline personality disorder (emotional variant) didn't help either. For the first hour of the session she cried hysterically. Only after she learned techniques like these she came to her senses and started to sob rather than cry out loud. And all that time I was laughing and feeling good to make sure she had an adequate reference to how she could start to feel.

The technique is called "spinning." No, you won't find it mentioned in most general books about NLP. It consists of two parts. The first is to stop the negative feeling. The second part is to start to feel good. If you actually practise the following steps, the results will follow. The steps are as follows:

STEP 1: Notice the place in your body where you feel bad. Is it your head, your chest, your belly or your arms and legs? Most of the time panic and fear attacks seem to rise up from the belly towards your head. Depressed feelings seem either located in your belly or in your chest. For most people finding these negative feelings is very easy. After all that is why they have come for help. If it is not easy

YOU,Unlimited 127

for them start to contrast the feeling against a memory of a time where you felt great. Ask yourself "How do I know that this is a happy memory and that the other feeling feels bad?" Notice where in your body you feel different. Feelings have to be in the body in order to be feelings. Our emotions are formed by "abusing" our sense of touch. Even if you feel strong emotional feelings in your body, this is nothing but brain activity that places this information into the raw sensory experience stream. Nothing is happening in the body itself.

Please note that sometimes people confuse secondary physical reactions with emotion. For instance, this is the case with anxiety attacks when your heart starts to beat faster, you might sweat and your hands might start to shake. We are less interested in these secondary physical reactions. The primary goal is to notice where the emotional feeling is situated. If you can close the loop of the feeling that is excellent.

STEP 2: Once you know where the feeling is located, notice in what way it is moving. I know beforehand that it is moving. This is because if it wasn't moving the emotion would die out. If you were to tap your hand in the same place over and over again, after some time you wouldn't feel the tap any more (your hand becomes numb) because your brain gets tired of the same signal over and over again. If your emotion doesn't die out quickly then there has to be some movement, some pattern that the feeling is following.

In most cases the feeling is either moving up or down, or circling clock or counter clockwise or forwards or backwards. Sometimes the feeling feels like a warm spot that is radiating from the inside out. If it seems that the feeling isn't moving than either you need to zoom in because you are sensing it at too high a level, or it is a kind of gnawing feeling pressuring from the outside in.

STEP 3: Once you have noticed the pattern your negative feeling follows put your two hands on your body and pull/push the feeling out of your body so that you can see it in front of you. (In case you have problems seeing the feeling, do the following: first imagine what colour your feeling would have. Because you cannot switch any of the senses off, each and every time you have a sensation your brain has a representation of the others senses, too. So when you think about it and guess what colour your feeling would have, what you actually do is just finding another way of representing your feeling more consciously. Once you have attributed a colour to the feeling, imagine a white paper in front of you. Imagine a colour crayon of the colour that your feeling has and start drawing the feeling on the white paper. Begin at the start and follow the pattern to the end and start all over again from there.)

It is important to notice that these techniques can't be done perfectly. They can only be done easily. At some time a client told me that she was unable to visualize her feelings because she didn't know what all the bones of the body looked like at that particular spot in her body. That's a little too much detail. Just some scratches and a few lines that make you see how the feeling moves.

STEP 4: Next step is to turn the pattern upside down so that the pattern now flows from the end towards the beginning. If you used the white paper trick from the previous step, just turn the paper upside down. Imagine what colour a good feeling would have and take out your imaginary crayon of that particular colour and just draw the same pattern again but now start at the end and move towards the beginning.

STEP 5: Once you see the pattern flowing the other way around take the feeling and put it back inside your body. Notice that the moment you put it back into your body, you feel the feeling starting to move in the opposite direction. It starts where it first ended and then moves on towards the old beginning. If you had made a loop of the feeling, the feeling will now be spinning in the opposite direction.

If you have trouble feeling the feeling this way, do the following: first feel your left hand (this is easy) and then change your focus to your right hand and feel that. Notice how easy that is. (This is due to the fact that your hand has a lot of nerves so your brain finds it easier to feel these locations. Once you can do this, feel how the feeling can go from your right hand all the way back to your left hand through your arms and shoulders by changing the focus of your mind.

If you can do that, just use the same principles to trace the feeling backwards through your body. So if it started in your belly and went up to your chest, just focus on your chest and then let your focus drop towards your belly.

STEP 6: Make sure that you are able to repeat to feel the feeling going into the opposite direction. Once you are able to repeat it easily, slowly but surely start to speed the feeling up by letting it go faster and faster through your body in the opposite direction. (With some people it works better if you slow it further down, but this is a very small minority.)

When you have done this for a couple of minutes notice that the bad feeling has strongly diminished or has vanished completely. Now it's important to quickly follow up with part two: to start to feel good for no reason at all.

PART 2: If you have done the previous steps in the right way, you should now be back in some kind of neutral state. Compare it with your memory of eating a slice of bread with peanut butter. I am sure that you remember a time you ate one, but that you have no emotional reaction (if there is one, choose something else that is silly).

Now that we have confused the brain cells enough to stop feeling bad it is a good idea to give them something to do. Most people have a thousand and one ways of feeling bad, and only one or two ways of feeling good, so it is important to fill your neutral state with a good feeling or your unconscious mind might take another bad feeling. You do this with the following steps:

STEP 1: Remember a time when you felt really good. It doesn't matter whether it is a moment when you felt really relaxed, or motivated or strong, whatever it is that you want (you can build a repertoire of good feelings this way anyway so that you have an appropriate good feeling for every occasion).

STEP 2: Once you know where and when you felt really good, just notice what the environment looked like and with whom you were there. If you see yourself in the picture, just float into your body and see what you saw, hear what you heard and feel what you felt. Feels good doesn't it?

STEP 3: Now notice where the good feeling starts and how its pattern moves through your body. If you find that your good feelings feel a lot weaker than your bad feelings, this is most common. Most people are experts at feeling bad but amateurs at feeling good. Luckily we are about to change this.

STEP 4: As soon as you have found the pattern or loop just continue to spin your feeling through it. Notice that if you speed up the spinning your feelings tend to grow stronger. As long as you keep spinning, the good feeling remains. If you want to feel good for no reason at all, just practise this technique a lot. Because there has to be no reason at all for you to relive the good moments in your past and feel good at present.

STEP 5: Test your work. Try to get the bad feeling back in vain. Notice how hard or impossible it has become to feel that particular bad feeling. Laugh at yourself for being so silly to fail at feeling bad and giggle.

Now it is smart not to look for bad feelings. Just use the technique to stop bad feelings reactively when you notice one. Just make sure that you become very intolerable towards bad feelings. It's much easier to stop them when they are small and barely noticeable than when they are strong and you endure them, thus letting them grow and grow and overwhelm you.

The technique for feeling good on the other hand can be done pro-actively whenever you want to feel good for no reason at all. Make sure that you practise feeling good for at least ten minutes each day for at least a period of two weeks, just to train your brain into a habit of feeling good rather than bad. But if I were you I wouldn't limit myself to just ten minutes. Why not a few hours or more each day?

DON'T SPEND TIME LOOKING FOR BAD THINGS IN YOUR PAST OR FUTURE

B ut what to do if the above technique only produces good feelings that last for a short time? In case you did the previous technique and were able to feel good, but only for a very short time, what happens is that your brain comes up with new things to feel bad about. Most of the time these are pictures of events either in the past or in the future. You could use the previous technique again to stop the bad feeling and start to feel good, but you would be very busy doing this all the time, as your brain just keeps popping up pictures that make you feel bad (or movies in case your picture has movement in it).

What is needed is a technique to stop these images from entering your consciousness and wasting all your time by making you feel bad about them. The same way we stopped feeling bad by unlearning the brain to follow a particular pattern, we must teach the brain cells involved with the bad picture production to stop putting these pictures into your mind.

The good thing about the past is that it is over. And as nobody owns a crystal ball, to gaze into the future to make you feel bad about yourself seems such a waste of time. Just imagine how you would feel if you didn't feel bad about the past or the future. And how much time you would have for wonderful things.

Just like the last technique with which we spun those bad feelings backwards, we have to come up with some technique to spin these pictures backwards. And this is precisely what we are going to do. We'll start with the past, because the technique to clear the past only uses the first half of the technique for the future. So there is some overlap we can use. Here's what you do:

STEP 1: Somehow you are reliving some ugly event from the past that you cannot get out of your head. This is human, all too human. But at least comfort yourself into knowing that this unpleasant happening had an end. At some point of time it was over. Now this doesn't have to be the moment where it technically ended, but it is more the moment this bad period ended for you emotionally (if you are in the middle just take the present as the end point). At some point in time, I know you let out a big sigh and felt relieved that it was all behind you. That is the moment I am looking for.

STEP 2: Once you know which moment for you meant the end, I want you to go back in time and remember what you looked like. Make sure that you create a still picture in your mind. So if you were reliving a certain period make sure that the movie of this period has ended in the still picture of you sighing out of relief.

STEP 3: The next step is to take this still picture of you feeling relieved and turn it into black and white. Just like an old black and white photograph.

STEP 4: After you have turned the picture into black and white, hear a silly tune. What really works well is circus music, but any silly tune will do.

STEP 5: Once you have a black and white picture and hear the silly tune, the next thing to do is to rewind the whole movie of the bad period to the starting point. Do it quickly. Sometimes it helps to start slowly and just see everything going backwards. People moving backwards, words going backwards, everything in reverse. Repeat it, but this time do it faster and faster.

Again, these are techniques that you can't do perfectly, only easily. Just remember what it looked like when you were rewinding old VCR tapes. The pictures aren't that clear, and it is okay to miss some parts. We'll check how well it worked afterwards.

STEP 6: Again test your work. Think back to the bad time and notice that your emotions are no longer triggered. It is not that you don't know that bad things didn't happen, you still do, but the bad feelings associated with them are gone. It's the same neutral feeling that you had with the peanut butter sandwich.

What happened is that, again, you confused your brain cells. The original memory was coded in colour with normal sounds, going from the beginning to the end at a normal pace. Now you ran the same memory in black and white, with silly music and in reverse quickly! No wonder the brain cells simply give up to connect the bad feeling to it.

In case the bad feeling has almost gone but not completely, simply run this technique a few more times. Your brain will pick up all that is needed to learn. In cases where the bad feeling is not reduced greatly, just run the previous technique before you do this one. Spin the bad feeling in the opposite way and as soon as you notice the bad feeling losing strength, rewind the film of the event backwards in black and white with a silly tune at high speed. Afterwards use the technique to spin a good feeling to make sure that all the brain cells involved now make you feel good.

If you worry too much about the future you basically do the same. When worrying you kind of run negative scenarios through your mind. These scenarios are like little movies. What you do is that you'll watch them for the last time but make sure that you'll watch them all the way to the end as not leave any negativity behind when you start rewinding them. If you are not sure whether you have found the end just ask yourself what's so bad about this that you worry about it. Any answer but "this is bad enough in itself" means you are extending the scenario in your mind.

Once you have seen the end of the scenario, notice that you will probably be relieved that it is over. No matter how bad the imagined event, you know that you will get over it. (Only if you worry about dying this works a little bit different. Just see yourself in heaven as described by your own religious beliefs) Once you have realized what you look like when you are relieved that the bad times are over, take that image and just run the exercise as described above but add the following steps. Because the future is still open, it is undecided. Unlike the past in which case it is handy to live in the same shared reality as the people who where there at the time, nobody knows what your future will hold. Not you, not me, not your doctor. Even with "certain" things like gravity, seemingly real and universal, there is no guarantee that it'll work tomorrow just the way as it did today. It is very probable, but not certain. Most people who hold so called "realistic" views on what the future will be like, really have a negative outlook only. This negative outlook is as unrealistic as a positive outlook as we don't know what the future will hold for us. Who would have thought that the Berlin Wall would be torn down by a second rate actor who became, as many feel, a first class president? Given that one outlook isn't more realistic than any other, it's best to choose the outlook that is healthiest for you and that is a positive one.

STEP 7: After rewinding the bad film back to the beginning from the end in black and white with a silly tune at high speed, the next thing you do is to imagine a big white movie screen in front of you.

STEP 8: On this movie screen you are going to project a feel good movie in which you are the star! Just see yourself going through the motions of the event of feeling good. See yourself acting relaxed and strong. See yourself motivated and feeling good. It is as if you had a magic wand and you could see yourself acting precisely the way you want to. There is only one catch. You can only change your behaviour and nothing else. A beautiful example when this went horribly wrong was with a client of mine (type VIII, the boss, borderline impulsive variant) who had a lot of stress about his printing business going broke. He physically collapsed at work, and developed many phobias and felt depressed. Working with him I taught him this technique. After the first time I did this with him, he lit up like a candle. Knowing that most of the time type VIII doesn't react so strongly to these techniques I immediately asked him what he had done in his mind.

He told me that he just saw himself buying a lottery ticket and that he won ten million dollars, immediately ending his financial woes. This works great of course but only for a very short time because if he would have bought the lottery ticket he would have won much less and the trouble would start all over again. (Lotteries are a special income-tax for people who are bad at mathematics.)

STEP 9: Always test your work, also in this case. Just think about the event that had you worried and see what film pops up in your mind. If you did it correctly you will notice that the new feel good movie is the one that pops up.

Again only use this technique reactively when you are wasting too much time (like any time) on future events. There is no need to go out and look for trouble. Just feeling good and seeing what a wonderful future is ahead of you suffice.

MAKE NEGATIVE
THOUGHTS
RIDICULOUS

I hope you realize that we now have taken care of negative feelings (sense of touch) and bad imagery (sense of sight). One major sense remains, namely our sense of hearing. This sense is used by the brain for creating conscious thoughts. It is as if you hear your own voice talking to you, the so called inner dialogue. Don't freak about hearing voices. Just because psychologists and psychiatrists never think and hence never hear their own voices, they have become a bit suspicious about hearing voices. Ignore it, it's completely normal. It's called thinking and remembering what people sound like.

Unfortunately now and then a negative thought pops up in your mind and no matter how hard you try to push it away it tends to remain there and make you feel bad. As it turns out, trying to stop negative thoughts is next to impossible. This is just the way our brain works. If I tell you not to think about a pink elephant now, guess what pops up in your mind? Right, a pink elephant. Even for those who are very fast and saw a purple elephant with dots, you still imagine an elephant. What happens is that you look at the pink elephant and then decide to change it. In order to understand the words you have to make the pictures. Humans just can't help themselves.

Luckily, there is a different way to make these negative thoughts go away. What you do is to make them ridiculous. Our brain just finds it very hard to keep thinking ridiculous thoughts. Somehow it is only interested in holding onto what seems real and really important. If it were otherwise, stand up comedians would have a much easier job. They would just have to tell one joke at the beginning of the show and people would laugh their heads off for the next hour or so. This is simply not how it works. The stand up comedian has to keep on telling jokes to keep you laughing.

As soon as a thought is found ridiculous it will disappear from our brain. There are basically two ways of achieving this. The first way is to listen carefully to the voice of the negative thought and notice that it is your own voice but with a negative and serious tone. What you do is this. Just keep on repeating the negative thought but while you keep repeating it, change the tone of voice to the most sexy voice you have. (I know, you don't have a sexy voice, but that was not what I asked for. I only said: "the most sexy voice you have". There is always one that is the best you can do).

So if for instance you thought "I'll never understand the value of the Enneagram with regard to NLP" with a negative and serious tone, just change it now to: "Oh ah, I'll never understand the value of the Enneagram with regard to NLP" (saying it to yourself in the most sexy voice you have).

The second way is well-known, or at least its ineffective version is. It's known as contrasting. When you are contrasting you usually compare your situation to that of someone who is worse off than you are. Unfortunately, most of the time it's done incorrectly. It's when people come up to you and tell you that whatever negative feeling that you experience "isn't bad at all, don't worry about it. Children in Africa are worse off." Remember the pink elephant? What you pick up from this sentence is that it is very bad indeed and that you should worry about it. The little children of Africa, who cares about them anyway. It's about you feeling bad, right? As you see, the complete opposite effect of what one had in mind. Well meant, but wrong effect.

Much better to do it the other way around. To anti-contrast. Just tell yourself the following: "It is completely right to feel these negative feelings. It's not like this situation isn't extremely terrible or something. And sure, those poor hungry kids in Africa wandering through the desert, sure, that kind of sucks too. But hell, it is in no way even comparable to what I experience. What is happening to me is much, much worse." What happens in your mind is that it will revolt against the very thought and dissolve the original negative thoughts you had. (If you find little hungry children in Africa a bit outdated, another favourite case of mine, the Tsunami victims, works well too. At least I think you get the message.)

HOW AND WHEN TO USE THESE NLP TECHNIQUES?

As you have seen by now, the Enneagram model presupposes that at certain times stress induces negative behaviour in us. This negative behaviour can either be classified as anger, fear or feeling bad. And it has a list of associated negative traits that you kind of borrow from other types.

What you do as soon as you notice that you are acting out these borrowed negative traits is STOP and realize that you are basically stressing. Next thing to do is to notice which of the senses is most dominant. Is it that you predominantly see negative images about the future or past, have negative thoughts or just feel bad? In the end it always comes down to feelings. If you looked at negative images but felt wonderful it would be ok. But some people are less inclined to notice their feelings as well as their imagery or thoughts (type V, the Analist for instance tends to have more problems feeling their emotions).

As soon as you have noticed the dominant sense, you use the technique for that sense to have the negativity disappear. Most of the time the bad feelings disappear. If not, just start over again but this time start with the technique to spin your bad feelings backwards first.

Please note that it is a bad idea to start looking for negative stuff. That would entail to training yourself to feel bad. Just use these techniques reactively, that means whenever you experience negativity. If, on the other hand, you want to do some things pro-actively, what you can do (and which in fact is a good idea) is to practise feeling good for no reason at all. This can be done, by just doing the second part of the spinning technique. Do this for at least ten minutes a day. This will train your brain to get good feelings faster and easier. By the way, don't let me hold you back to feel good for more than ten minutes a day, if you like feeling good rather than bad.

CONCLUSIONS

BY NOW I HOPE THAT YOU ARE AS CONVINCED OF THE VALUE OF
the Enneagram reconciled with NLP as I am. If you, like me, want
to be able to quickly note what kind of personality someone has,
start by learning from everyone you meet. Before you know it, you
will start to notice character traits more and more easily.

Once you are able to quickly establish someone's character by
both looking and listening very closely, or by asking them the
right questions, you can use that information for diagnosis and
building convincer states. In time you will learn which strategic
approach to each Enneagram type works best with that type (a
subject for a whole new book), so that you easily mind-read the
masses and act accordingly.

By combining the Enneagram with NLP, you not only know what to do better, but also know how to do it. An ability lacking in many change workers whether they call themselves therapists, coaches or trainers. In my view, telling someone that he or she has to do things differently without knowing and explaining them how to do it, is unethical. But once you have learned these skills you are well on your way to start improving your life and the lives of those around you considerably. When in two years' time you will look back to this moment in time, you'll realize that this was the moment that the real change had begun. You are most welcome.

THE INSTITUTE OF UNCONVENTIONAL WISDOM

ALL OF MY WORK FOR TIOUW.COM IS BASED ON THE IDEAS AND principles set out in this book. With the help of group sessions and one-on-one coaching I make sure my clients come to feel better and grow to replace their negative emotions with feelings of relaxation, personal power, and self-confidence.

I also provide numerous courses on the Enneagram and NLP such as "You, Unlimited" and the NLP Practitioner and Master Practitioner weekends.

To give you a better idea of all the things I do, and how I do them, I set up http://usa.tiouw.com especially for you. You will find PDFs on coaching, good advice on handling your relationships, and a set of guidelines assisting you to make the right choice for NLP courses. They are all free – for those people who live to unburden themselves and dare to hope for a future full of promise.

TIOUW.com: Unconventionally Better.

ABOUT THE AUTHOR

PEOPLE OFTEN ASK ME IF I MYSELF HAVE EXPERIENCED ALL kinds of things and if that is the very reason why I have started to do this work. Of course everyone's life is different but it certainly helps if you have had experience with this sort of business. That's why I think it is a good idea to introduce myself properly. So that you know a little bit what sort of person I am.

This is the reason why I openheartedly tell you about what I have experienced. Besides my own shortcomings that I ran into I also experience on a daily basis what has happened to other people.

It is my opinion that with a good insight into the person I am, it will be easier for you to decide whether or not to follow private sessions or workshops and seminars.

Some people don't realize this but I am busy giving private sessions all day long. I see hundreds of people a year. Whether it is about problems with fear, emotions or anger, I solve them every day. In the seminars I give I also meet a lot of people who I can teach to feel good in a relaxed and easy manner.

Don't be worried therefore if I will find your problem crazier than that of someone else or that it should be something to be ashamed of. In my vision one person is as crazy as the other. And it is not as much that something is wrong with you but that you have only learned something wrong at a difficult time

I won't start burrowing in the past at all. The beautiful thing about the past is that it is over. In the end it is about me teaching you how to feel better now. We'll gladly leave the past behind and focus on the present and the future again. In spite of this I will tell you something about my own past, so that you can see what I can mean for you.

My own story begins somewhere in the beginning of the nineties of the 20th century. At the university I discovered that I liked to work much more than to study. Teaching, organizing conferences and programming was much more fun than rummaging through dull books.

Immediately after my studies I worked for a very short time for a big programming firm. After a fortnight it occurred to me "my

God, I have to think of a way to get out of here". That's how much I liked it. Therefore, I am a strong advocate of doing a job that you really like.

Fortunately the nineties were a blessing for programmers. I acquired a big oilcompany for my employer and got my own department as thanks. I had promised to stay on for a year and so I did. After the fourth re-organization in one year I dedided by start on my own. In spite of ample raise of salary the gap between acquisition and my wages was too big.

My employer had sent me to every course they could think of. One was even more soporific than the other. And I mean this literally. My pub going will not have helped at all but o man how dull these courses were.

In my own business I had made up my mind not to follow any more courses. However, at the end of the nineties, affairs took another turn. Not only did I lose my first order, which made me doubt my sales abilities but I was also invited for a workshop by one of my biggest customers.

So as not to lose the client I arrived at the workshop acting as if I really enjoyed myself. I presupposed trying to stay awake for three days. But to my happy surprise this workshop turned out to be quite different. Sparkling, full of humour and fascinating from the first till the last minute.

After three days of the course I asked the course leader what made his course so fascinating and those others so soporific.

"NLP", he said. After that I immediately bought a number of books on NLP. All the wrong books by the wrong authors. But one of those authors wrote some tough stories about his trainer. One Richard Bandler.

I quickly got hold of some of his books. When I read those I thought: "Look, he is a man after my heart. Let's find out if he is still alive and if so if he still gives training." In both cases it was a positive. So off to the United States just like that.

Bandler's site looked like it had been clicked together by a teenager. (Later on I learned that this was actually so). Big flashing texts like "Be Happy Fast Now" and "Become Richer than your Competitor". I had no idea what to expect.

Somewhere at the back of my head I presupposed that I was one of the very few trying this out. Great was my surprise therefore when in the morning I had to file up behind about a hundred and fifty people. "At least I am not the only one doing this" was what I could think.

After five minutes however, a lot became clearer when I was sitting in the full hotel auditorium. Bandler started and the first thing I thought was "O shit, I should have known this when I was fifteen. How much misery with parents, friends but especially girl-friends I could have avoided if I had learned these techniques at that time." Fortunately, an elderly man comforted me with the thought that in your late twenties was still a lot younger that he in his fifty-fifth year and of course this is so. Every day still I consider myself fortunate that I was able to learn this trade and turn it into a fulltime job.

That I can do such a grateful job helping people to feel good and strong again in a very humouristic, easy and fun way.

Richard Bandler is a special man. I think I am rather intelligent myself, Grammar School, reading Philosophy at University. High marks. But when I met Richard Bandler for the first time, I realized that he truly is a genius. The wondrous things I saw that man do. Nearly everything I do, I learned from him.

He had me certified as international NLP trainer. Advanced NLP Master practition and Neuro-Hypnotic Repatterning. Moreover, I am a member of The Society of NLP and the NVNLP. Therefore I am proud to bear the official seal of The Society of NLP. But the most important thing is my unfailling care for my clients. My zeal to make sure that everything will be all-right again. There is no guarantee beforehand but fortunately very many people are doing well.

FREE AUDIO BONUS

FREE AUDIO RECORDING OF JOOST VAN DER LEIJ, INTERNATIONAL NLP & THE ENNEAGRAM TRAINER

"HOW TO STOP ANY NEGATIVE FEELINGS AND FEEL GOOD
for no reason at all"

You have read the book, and the most central technique for a better life is to be able to stop any negative feelings. However, reading about it is one thing but listening step by step to guidance by a master trainer is a whole different ball game.

Listen to Joost van der Leij as he coaches you through the feel good exercises and how he makes sure that you feel a whole lot better.

Download recording at http://usa.tiouw.com/bonus

9 781600 373572